The Kind Leader

The Kind Leader

A Practical Guide to Eliminating Fear, Creating Trust, and Leading with Kindness

Karyn Ross

CRC Press is an imprint of the
Taylor & Francis Group, an informa business

First published 2022
by Routledge
600 Broken Sound Parkway #300, Boca Raton FL, 33487

and by Routledge
2 Park Square, Milton Park, Abingdon, Oxon OX14 4RN

Routledge is an imprint of the Taylor & Francis Group, an informa business

Library of Congress Cataloging-in-Publication Data
A catalog record for this title has been requested

ISBN: 978-0-367-69343-5 (hbk)
ISBN: 978-0-367-69342-8 (pbk)
ISBN: 978-1-00-314143-3 (ebk)

DOI: 10.4324/9781003141433

Typeset in Garamond
by Newgen Publishing UK

Contents

Preface

The best kind of leader is a Kind Leader.

Karyn Ross

Why I Decided to Write a Book about Kindness in Leadership

I can't say that I ever expected to write a book about kind leadership. Yet, here I am, doing just that. Now, you very well may be asking yourself, "If Karyn never thought she'd write a book about kind leadership, why is she writing one? And why now?" So, here's the answer.

Because it's what's needed.

Perhaps, like me you've noticed an increase in unkindness in the last few years. In politics, as we've seen from recent elections in different countries, world leaders and political candidates don't seem to think twice about bad-mouthing and ridiculing other candidates and their followers. On the streets of our cities and neighborhoods, people with differing sets of beliefs clash, repeating the unkind words and sentiments they've heard from their leaders. Sometimes these clashes turn violent.

Walk into many work environments, and you won't have to wait too long to experience unkindness. Leaders complain about workers, coworkers complain about colleagues and client service representatives speak unkindly about customers. Senior leaders and lower level managers regularly treat workers in disrespectful, unkind ways. And this has only been magnified by the COVID-19 pandemic.

Finally, we're inundated with unkindness at home. On television shows, twenty-four-hour news programs and social media platforms we're exposed over and over again to unkindness. Whether it's about a political leader and their policies, reality TV, true-life crime series, to social media feeds filled with unkind words and even unkinder memes, wherever we are, it seems we're awash in a media sea of unkindness.

Day after day, as I reflected on the examples of organizational and workplace unkindness people told me about and on the rampant unkindness that I saw on television and social media, I realized that there was a common thread that ran through them. And that common thread was leadership. The words and actions of unkind leaders – politically and organizationally – seemed to influence others to follow suit. So, I did a little research on the internet. And what I found out is that although there are a large number of books and articles written on many different aspects of leadership, very few are written on kindness and leadership.

So, I decided to write one.

Because, as the founder and president of The Love and Kindness Project Foundation, a coach and consultant to leaders at all levels around the world, and as a person who is just as negatively affected by unkind leadership as everyone else, I'm not prepared to sit back and just do nothing. And I'm guessing by the fact that you've chosen this book, you aren't prepared to either. Which brings me to …

Who This Book Is For!

You!

This book is written for you. To help you become a kinder leader and help others become kinder leaders as well. Because whether you have a formal leadership role or not, and think of yourself as a leader or not, as you'll see shortly, everyone is a leader at some point. And as a leader, the way *you* think, speak and act – both kindly and unkindly – has a huge effect on others.

Perhaps you're thinking to yourself, "Leadership and kindness are something you're born with. They're simply personality traits that aren't changeable." Or perhaps you're worried that it's going to be difficult to change. That little voice inside your head is saying, "I've done things the same way for a long time. I'm too old to change." If you are, please stop. Because as was found in the longest personality study undertaken anywhere in the world, published in 2016 in *Psychology and Aging*, personality isn't immutable. It changes over the course of one's lifetime.[1]

You can – and will – learn, grow and change over a lifetime. You can improve your leadership and become kinder at any point in your life. And doing that will influence others to be kinder as well.

Thank you for buying and reading this book.

And most importantly, thank you for your leadership and your help in creating a kinder world for all of us!

With love and kindness,
Karyn Ross

Note

1 M. A. Harris, C. E. Brett, W. Johnson, and I. J. Deary. Personality Stability from Age 14 to Age 77 Years. *Psychology and Aging*, 31(8) (2016): 862–874. https://doi.org/10.1037/pag0000133

With Kind Thanks

Writing this book wouldn't have been possible without the kindness and contributions of many people!

First of all, special thanks to all those who contributed the stories, experiences and reflections on kind leadership that you will read throughout this book. This book wouldn't exist without all of you! In chapter order, kind thanks to:

Michelle Jorgensen, Amir Ghannad, Ann Howell, Deondra Wardelle, Jim Semple, James Hanson, Cheryl Jensen, Debbie Eison, Petrina McGrath, Craig Delmage, Gretchen Dieter, Grace Bourke, Lili Boyanova, Skip Steward, Dorota Jasielska, Glen Weppler, Kathi Littman, Pennie Saum, Karidja Sakanogo, Jamie Flinchbaugh, Michelle Hlywa, Doug Wotherspoon, Stewart Bellamy, Leslie Henckler, Linda Michelle Cohen. Noah Goellner, Stéfany Oliver and Matthew Grant.

Thank you to Leslie Henckler, my friend, mentor, kind leader and fabulous copy-editor for reading and doing the first edits of this manuscript. Your kindness and help over so many years are appreciated more than words can say!

A special thank you to my husband, Brian Hoffert (also known as Mr. Photoshop) for turning my drawings into the beautiful graphics you'll see throughout this book! A picture is worth a thousand words and I couldn't have brought my 'vision' to life without his help!

Much thanks to my editor Michael Sinocchi and to everyone at Productivity Press for supporting this book and turning my idea into a reality!

Finally, a huge thank you to you: The person reading this book. Thank you for choosing to learn about a better, kinder way to lead. Your kind leadership practice will change the world for the better for all of us.

With Kind Thanks

[illegible]

Chapter 1

Isn't Kindness a Sign of Weakness?

Kindness is not a sign of weakness. It is a sign of confidence.

Colin Powell, retired four-star general and former US Secretary of State

Discussion: Kind Leader Theory and Ideas for You to Think About

As discussed in the introduction, on the surface, the words 'leadership' and 'kindness' don't seem to go together. When I began telling people that I was going to write a book about kind leadership, I was met with a barrage of questions: Isn't leadership about 'strength'? About making tough decisions and having the fortitude to carry those decisions out no matter how difficult they are? And what about kindness? Isn't kindness a type of weakness? Don't kind people get walked all over? If leaders are too kind, how will they be able to make those inevitably tough decisions when the time comes? All great questions, and just the fact that people were asking them was hugely helpful in providing insight into some of the reasons kindness isn't the first word that comes to mind when most people think about leadership.

DOI: 10.4324/9781003141433-1

To make sure everyone reading is on the same page about these concepts, let's get started by defining 'leadership' and 'kindness' as they will be used throughout the book.

Defining Leadership

Leadership is a huge topic! Often discussed and widely written about, when I typed 'leadership books' into the search box on Amazon.com it took less than a second for 80,000 results to be returned! As I scanned through the results, I found books on leadership theory from different countries and historical periods, books on leadership strategy and tactics, books on how to improve personal leadership, books on leading teams, books on leading organizations, books on leading a country, and many more categories. With so many books on leadership (and if there are this many books on leadership, imagine how many articles there are), it's not surprising that definitions of what leadership is, what leaders do, and how they should do it, vary immensely.

For this book, I'm going to use a very simple definition of leadership:

Leaders lead other people.

At its most simple and basic definition, *a leader is a person who has at least one person following them*. Leadership doesn't have to be fancy and formal, and a leader doesn't have to have millions, thousands or even tens of followers. A leader is simply a person that *someone, in a moment of time, is following*. That person, the follower, *has decided to pay attention to, take their cues about how to act and react from, and have their thoughts, words and actions influenced by, a person they deem as 'leader'*.

Throughout each day, at work, at home and out in the community, each of us is constantly changing roles from leader to follower and back again. I call this swapping *Leader and Follower Hats*. Think about a typical day you or one of your colleagues and might have. In the morning, as you get your kids organized, ready for school and out the door, you're wearing your Leader Hat. Once you're at work, you've got your Follower Hat on as you listen to your manager read the daily key messages and set the work priorities. In the afternoon, you switch back to your Leader Hat as you mentor a new team member, then, an hour later, you switch back to your Follower Hat as you attend your organization's quarterly town hall. During the evening, while you coach your kids' soccer team, you put your Leader Hat back on.

Because followers take their cues about how to think, speak and act from leaders, it's important to recognize that *you are a leader*. That means leading with kindness isn't just something that politicians, CEO's, managers and supervisors need to practice and model. Everyone does! To do that, the first step is to become conscious of when you are wearing your Leader Hat and when you are wearing your Follower Hat. You'll find an exercise to do that (1.1) in the Practice Section on page 11. You can stop and do the exercise now or wait until you've finished this Discussion section.

Next, let's talk about kindness.

Defining Kindness

Like leadership, kindness means many things to many different people. I found that out not just by looking up the definition of kindness in a variety of online dictionaries, but through interviews I had with twenty-eight people who very kindly agreed to share their views on – and experiences with – kindness and leadership. As part of the interview, I asked people for their definition of kindness. Across the wide variety of answers I received, the words 'empathy' and 'compassion' came up over and over again. So, before defining kindness specifically, let's look at what empathy and compassion are. Then we'll discuss how they relate to kindness.

Empathy

Empathy is defined as "The ability to sense other people's emotions, coupled with the ability to imagine what someone else might be thinking or feeling".[1] Empathy is commonly described as being able to 'walk a mile in someone else's shoes' and to think about what someone else is experiencing and feeling, even if you are not in that exact situation. When you feel upset and angry after speaking with a co-worker who feels that they have been treated unjustly, you are feeling empathy. And when you feel pride in a job well done by your partner, spouse or child, you are feeling empathy as well.

Many of you may be familiar with the concept of empathy from the work done by Daniel Goleman on emotional intelligence in the 1990s. Part of a group of five non-technical skills, Goleman taught that empathy (along with self-awareness, self-regulation, motivation and social skill) and emotional intelligence was hugely important in enhancing a leader's performance. Especially at higher levels of leadership. For leaders in a business setting, Goleman explains that empathy doesn't just mean understanding the feelings of others' but "empathy means thoughtfully *considering* employees feelings – along with other factors – in the process of making intelligent decisions".[2] Goleman also explained that although empathy has a genetic component and is "born largely in the neurotransmitters of the brain's limbic system"[3], along with the other emotional intelligence skills, it can be taught and improved through conscious and deliberate practice and with feedback from others such as a coach.

Although Goleman doesn't explicitly talk about the relationship between empathy and kindness in his original work on emotional intelligence, later, in a blog post for his book *Force for Good*, Goleman states that "Research finds that compassion has better results than a tough-guy stance. For starters, people like and trust bosses who show kindness – and that in turn boosts their performance".[4]

Compassion

So, what's the difference between empathy and compassion? And why are both needed?

Like empathy, science has shown that compassion, "a sense of concern that arises when we are confronted with another's suffering and feel motivated to see that suffering relieved",[5] is hard-wired into the human brain. At an early age, children show the first signs of compassion when they reach out to hug another child who has fallen and skinned their knee. Later on, as teenagers, their upset and anger at perceived injustice to others that they see in their classrooms, on television and through social media, turns into a wish to 'do something to help'. Later on, those compassionate feelings manifest at work, when a colleague's family suffers a tragedy such as losing their house in a fire or having a family member diagnosed with a terminal illness. The feeling of compassion for their suffering is what motivates efforts to help such as collecting donations of clothing and household goods and sending group or company-wide cards, flowers and messages of caring.[6]

As adults, compassion is what connects feelings of empathy to acts of kindness to relieve the pain and suffering of those around us. Empathy is what allows you to think and feel 'outside' your own experience. Compassion for the difficult situation that another is in is what motivates you to move beyond 'feeling' to doing. As Thupten Jinpa, founder of the Compassion Institute says, "Compassion is what connects the feeling of empathy to acts of kindness, generosity, and other expressions of altruistic tendencies".[7]

Which brings us to kindness.

Kindness

When I interviewed people for this book, one of the first questions I asked was "How do you define kindness?" Over and over again, I found the same thing. That the people I interviewed didn't have an immediate answer. They had to stop and think about it. Sometimes for quite a while. When I asked why they were struggling, almost everyone had the same answer: that while they could easily describe a way someone acted that they defined as kind, defining 'kindness' itself was something that they hadn't thought about. After some thought, when they answered, I noticed three themes that crossed most people's definition of kindness.

The first was the idea of action. That kindness isn't simply about 'feeling', but about 'doing something'. As you can see from these definitions: "Kindness is trying to make somebody's day better"[8] (Cheryl Jensen, Higher Education leader) and "Kindness is doing things that make others feel, or become better" (James H. Hanson, M.D., Lean Healthcare Practice Director).[9] Over and over again, the idea of 'action' and words like 'doing' were repeated.

The second was that kindness focuses on others. That the 'action' and 'doing' inherent in kindness is directed outside of the self to other individuals and/or groups. A couple of examples of the many definitions that included this dimension are: "Do unto others as you would have them do unto you. Kindness means you can't be self-absorbed"[10] (Deondra Wardelle, business owner and human resources leader) and "Kindness means being considerate, giving, helping, doing kind things for others" (Dorota Jasielska, professor and researcher).[11] The word and concept of 'others' appeared in definition after definition.

The third was positivity. That the action undertaken was meant to create a positive effect and a beneficial outcome for the person that it is focused on. We can see that in these definitions: "Kindness is doing the right thing. It's genuine caring for the well-being of others and showing it"[12] (Jim Semple, manufacturing leader) and "Kindness is an act that benefits others as an end in itself" (Ann Howell, leadership coach).[13] In order to be defined as 'kindness', actions need to focus on positive benefit and outcome for someone else.

Putting these three themes – or dimensions – together, I created the definition of kindness that will be used throughout the rest of this book:

Kindness is an* action *(or set of actions), connecting a person's internal feelings of* empathy *and* compassion *to* others *that is undertaken with the purpose of generating a* positive *effect and outcome for another.

As you can see, all three dimensions – action, focusing on others and generating a positive effect and outcome – are included. Kindness isn't just about theoretically thinking about what it would be like to be in someone else's shoes. And it's not about feeling motivated to do something to help another person out. It's about actually doing the things that help someone else and have a positive effect and outcome for them. (In Chapters 4, 5 and 6, you'll learn how to do this as a leader through specific ways to think, speak and act kindly.)

Finally, defining kindness as actions that connect one person's thoughts and feelings to others with the purpose of generating a positive outcome

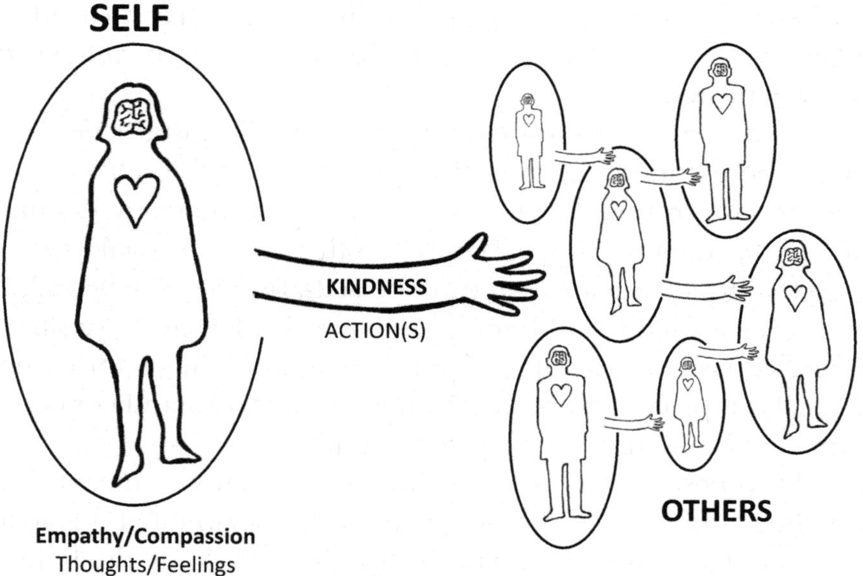

Figure 1.1 Kindness connects leaders to followers through positive action.

for the other person is unbelievably important when combined with the definition of leadership discussed earlier. Both because *leaders lead other people* by modeling ways to act and react, kind and not, and because followers take their cues from and are influenced by their leaders' words and actions, kind and not. And because everyone – *including you* – is a leader, the choice and practice of leading with kindness has a huge effect on whether the effects and outcomes generated for others are positive or not.

Assumptions, Systems and Models Frame Thoughts, Feelings and Actions

At this point you might be saying to yourself, "All of this is well and good, but still, isn't kindness a sign of weakness? Don't leaders need strength to lead people and to get results? Taking others' feelings into account when making decisions and acting for the good of others is a nice idea, but don't 'nice guys' (and nice leaders!) finish last?"

If this is what you're thinking, I'm not surprised, and I don't blame you! Because for many years, this is what people who have studied leadership, gone through MBAs, and read leadership books and articles have been taught. And people who haven't undertaken formal leadership studies have worked in organizations where those leadership values have permeated the organization. Where employees' feelings haven't been considered in leadership decisions, and where it has been clear that actions taken aren't going to have a positive effect on those being led, only on those who are leading.

It's important to remember that every person's beliefs and understanding are influenced by many factors: genetic makeup, individual temperament, cultural background, upbringing, education, experiences and a whole lot more. What you believe and why you believe it didn't just happen. You are exposed to many systems and models, each of which produces a wide variety of assumptions. And those assumptions, systems and models frame and influence your thoughts, feelings and actions. Including those about leadership, kindness and their relationship to each other.

I was talking about the assumption that leadership and kindness aren't compatible because leadership is associated with strength, and kindness with weakness, with my friend, client and holistic dentistry practice leader Michelle Jorgensen. After thinking about it for a little while, Michelle suggested that in her experience because men are more often thought of as 'natural leaders' and that kindness is a trait more commonly associated with women, 'leadership' and 'kindness' don't seem to go together. Michelle went on to say that at times, in order to be seen as a leader, she felt that she needed to suppress her desire to act in an empathic, compassionate and kind way as she didn't want to be seen as too 'weak' or 'feminine'. In order to be perceived as a leader, she felt that she had to 'act like a man' so she could be perceived as having the 'male' leadership quality of strength.[14]

Research backs up Michelle's experience. According to a 2018 research study on gender and leadership emergence led by Katie Badura and Emily Grijalva, PhD from the University at Buffalo, which spanned more than 19,000 participants across 136 studies and 59 years, found that "On average, men are more likely than women to emerge as leaders".[15] The researchers attributed the gap to "societal pressures that contribute to gender differences in personality traits. For example, men tend to be more assertive and dominant, whereas women tend to be more communal, cooperative and nurturing. As a result, men are more likely to participate and voice their opinions during group discussions and be perceived by others as leaderlike".[16] The researchers further went on to show that a focus on caring and positive outcomes for others wasn't associated with leadership: "Showing sensitivity and concern for others – stereotypically feminine traits – made someone less likely to be seen as a leader ... however, it's those same characteristics that make leaders effective".[17]

As Michelle experienced, the underlying systems and models that you are exposed to create a framework that contributes to the way you perceive things, including your thoughts around what leadership looks like, and what it doesn't. It also affects the way you act and react. As you work through this book, understanding the systems and models that you currently use to frame leadership is extremely important. You'll find an exercise to help you do that in this chapter's Practice Section (Figure 1.4) on page 12. (You can stop and do the exercise now or continue reading and do it at the end of this chapter.)

If current models of leadership positively associate strength, and other similar qualities such as assertiveness and dominance with leadership, and kindness is associated with weakness, what can be done to change the perception that leadership and kindness can't go together? How can kindness and leadership become associated? And, most importantly, is kindness really a sign of weakness? Because as Amir Ghannad, author of *The Transformative Leader* says, "Although kindness is often thought of as a weakness, it takes a lot of strength to consider others' needs".[18]

Change the Outcome by Changing the Model

General Colin Powell, a retired four-star general who served as the Chairman of the Joint Chiefs of Staff of the US Army, the United States' National Security Advisor and the US Secretary of State, doesn't see kindness as weakness. Or incompatible with strong leadership. In fact, in his book It *Worked for Me*, Powell devotes an entire chapter to kindness!

Throughout the chapter, by relating stories from his service as an Episcopalian minister, military roles and tenure as Secretary of State, General Powell shows the benefits of acting with kindness. Echoing Daniel Goleman's work on empathy and emotional intelligence, General Powell says, "If you have developed a reputation for kindness and consideration, then even the most unpleasant decisions will go down easier because everyone will understand why you are doing what you are doing. They will realize that your decision must be necessary, and is not arbitrary or without empathy".[19]

If a four-star general like Colin Powell can associate kindness with strength and leadership, then the rest of us can too!

People Create Models and Systems

The way to get started associating kindness and leadership is to create new models that bring them together. Although it may seem that the models and systems you experience are static, in truth, models and systems change all the time. Before the ancient Greeks figured out that the world was round, people thought it was flat! Democracy and capitalism are newer government and economic models. Leadership and management models change all the time too. Lean leadership and agile management are just two of the newer models that come to mind.

And new models aren't created out of thin air. They are created by people. People who have new ideas based on the different backgrounds, experiences and perceptions they have. People like New Zealand Prime Minister Jacinda Ardern, who has one of the best track records leading her country through the coronavirus crisis because of her focus on leading with kindness. In an October 2020 interview with *Meridian* magazine, Ms. Ardern said, "We teach kindness, empathy and compassion to our children, but then, somehow, when it comes to political leadership, we want a complete absence of that. So, I am trying to chart a different path. That will attract critics – but I can only be true to myself".[20] By being true to herself, and leading with kindness, Ms. Ardern is creating a new model. Not only in theory, but in practice.

That is what this book is about.

Creating a new model for kind leadership. And not just a theoretical model, but a system to practice it. Because in order to create a kinder world – to change the unkind outcomes currently experienced by so many at work, in their communities and around the globe – what is needed are leaders who model the three dimensions of kindness: action, focus on others, and positive effect.

Practice: Practical Exercises to Use to Turn Your Thoughts into Action

Theory in itself won't help you become a kinder leader or change the world for the kinder. Putting the ideas espoused by a theory or model into practice will. The three exercises in this chapter are designed to make you aware of the current assumptions you have about leadership and kindness.

Exercise 1: Recognizing When I'm a Leader and When I'm a Follower

As you go about your day, you switch back and forth between your Leader Hat and your Follower Hat. Use this exercise to help you (and others) see when you are wearing each.

When do I wear my Leader Hat and when do I wear my Follower Hat?
Share examples from individual, family, community and work situations

I wear my Leader Hat when I'm...	I wear my Follower Hat when I'm...

Figure 1.2 Making when I'm a leader and when I'm a follower visible.

Exercise 2: Seeing How I'm Leading with Kindness Now

There are probably many times when you are wearing your Leader Hat that you are already turning thoughts and feelings (empathy and compassion) into actions that create positive effects and outcomes for others. Use this exercise to help you become conscious of when you are leading with kindness now! What opportunities might you have missed?

How have I turned empathy and compassion into kindness? Write examples from situations you have been in as a leader at work, home and community				
Situation	Empathy (What I thought)	Compassion (What I felt)	Kindness (Action(s) I took)	Positive effect for the other person

Figure 1.3 Kindness is about turning thoughts and feelings into action(s) that positively affect others.

Exercise 3: Making the Models That Frame My Thoughts and Actions Visible

Making the models that frame and influence your thoughts about leadership and kindness visible will help you become more conscious of what is influencing your thoughts, feelings, actions and reactions.

What models frame my thoughts and actions about leadership and kindness? List business, religious, political and other models that are important to you.	
List business, religious, political models	**How I act and react based on the Model**

Figure 1.4 Models frame and influence thoughts, actions and reactions.

Reflection: What Would You Do? Kind Leader Practice Scenarios

Now that you've had the opportunity to read the ideas and theory presented in the Discussion section and do the Practice exercises, it's time to reflect on what you've learned and proactively plan how to apply those learnings in situations you will encounter. Obviously, you are reading this book because you want to be a kinder leader. However, it is also important to put on your Follower Hat when reflecting and thinking about application, because as a Follower, you have the ability to choose the way you react to your leader's words and actions. Your reaction can help them become kinder leaders as well!

To get the most of this part of the book, read the situation, reflect on it using the theory and ideas from the Discussion section and then write about what you would do in that situation. There are no 'right' or 'wrong' answers, and every person will write a different ending. Use this opportunity to finish Kay'La Janson's and Kevin Landrell's stories in the kindest way possible.

A Tale of Two First Days

Scenario 1 – Kay'La's Story: Does It Really Have to be 'Unkind' at the Top?

Kay'La Janson was super-excited. She was also a little (well maybe a lot) nervous too. Today was her first day on the job as CEO of Codstom Industries, a multinational organization that provided customer service outsourcing. Codstom had been in business for about 65 years, and although they had been very successful in past, over the last couple of years, with the advent of new and improved technologies and intensified competition from competitors around the world, business wasn't exactly booming. The 'retirement' of the previous CEO was quite abrupt and had caused a lot of speculation within and outside the organization. Rumors were rampant and those who had left the company had posted some pretty unpleasant and unkind things on social media.

Kay'La was optimistic though. She trusted that her work as a Vice President at one of Codstom's largest competitors had prepared her for the challenge of turning Codstom around. She knew the industry, she knew the market and she knew some of the problems Codstom had been having. And not just the financial 'business' problems. The culture problems as well. Codstom's reputation as being a cut-throat, dog-eat-dog work environment was well known. From the vanquished CEO on down, Codstom leaders were hired and promoted for their ability to get results, no matter what and no matter how. And it seemed to have worked, at least on the surface, until now. "It's going to be a challenge to turn this around", Kay'La thought to herself as she got out of her car in the parking lot of Codstom's headquarters. "But that's okay, because the one thing I love more than anything else is a challenge. And I truly believe that people can change, and that, as a leader, how I act, and what I model, will be the foundation of that change. I was hired for my belief that kind leadership will turn Codstom around and I know that the best way to deal with unkindness is to be kind. It's going to be a great first day, because no matter what happens, the best time to get change started is right now!"

Heading into the building, Kay'La passed a number of people wearing Codstom badges. Some were heading in, others out, on their way home. Kay'La smiled and said a cheery hello to everyone she passed. She was surprised to find that no one, not a single person, looked up, smiled or returned her greeting. The just rushed past, head down. "That's interesting", Kay'La thought to herself. "I wonder who will meet me at the door?" To her surprise, no one did. So Kay'La got into the elevator, pushed the button for the fifth floor and headed for where she assumed her office would be. Opening the door, she saw her administrative assistant sitting at a large desk. "Good morning, I'm Kay'La Janson", she said, with an outstretched hand. "You must be Anderson. I've been looking forward to meeting you!" To Kay'La's surprise, Anderson didn't accept her offer of a handshake, and instead just turned back to his computer and started typing. As Kay'La walked into her office, she said quietly to herself, "Well, at least I know what I'm up against. I think the first thing that I will do is…"

Now It's Your Turn to Reflect and Apply

Put on your Leader Hat and think about how you would react to Anderson and what you would do next. What would be the first steps you would take to model kind leadership for the rest of the organization? Write your ideas here:

Scenario 2 – Kevin's Story: 'You Can't Teach an Old Customer Service Rep New Tricks'… Can You?

Kevin Landrell was excited and nervous too. He had been a team member at Codstom Industries for the past five years. As a customer service representative, he had the opportunity to hear how frustrated Codstom's customers were with many of their services and processes. And he'd also heard the surly replies from some of the other customer service representatives, and the unkind things they said about their customers when they hung up the phone. Since joining Codstom, Kevin had worked for a succession of supervisors. Most weren't very friendly and some even joined in on the gossip and added their snide remarks about customers who complained. And most of Kevin's supervisors hadn't been that helpful either. If they weren't in a meeting when he needed help, most of Kevin's inquiries or suggestions of how to satisfy customers and make things better fell on deaf ears. Luckily, though, Kevin had one supervisor who was different. One who always had time to listen to his questions, who gave him a lot of encouragement and always had a kind word for customers. It had made a huge impression on Kevin and given him the motivation and aspiration to become a supervisor himself. "And today's the day", Kevin said as he looked in the mirror as he got ready for work! "I finally made it! I'm going to be able to 'pay it forward' and put all the things I learned from my former supervisor into practice!"

When Kevin got to his new, much-larger, supervisor's cubicle, his team's early shift was already busy taking calls. He could hear Molly, one of the customer service rep's voices getting louder and louder. Kevin walked out of his cubicle toward her just as he heard her say, "You can complain as much as you want, but it's not going to make any difference … and no … you can't speak with my supervisor …" Then Molly hung up the phone, and as she turned to Jaden, who sat next to her, with a smirk on her face, Kevin intervened and …

Now It's Your Turn to Reflect and Apply

If you were in Kevin's place, what would you do? With your Leader Hat on, how would you approach Molly and start to break the cycle of unkindness?

Chapter 1 Kind-Points

- *Leaders lead other people.* A leader is a person who has at least one other person following them. A follower is a person who has decided to pay attention to, take their cues about how to act, and be influenced by the person they deem as a leader.
- *People switch between being leaders and followers.* Throughout the day, depending on the situation, you switch between being a leader and being a follower.
- *Empathy and compassion are related to kindness.* They are the internal 'thinking and feeling' part of how you understand and feel others' experiences, difficulties and what motivate you to want to help.
- *Kindness connects leaders to followers through positive action(s).* 'Kindness is an action (or set of actions), connecting a person's internal feelings of empathy and compassion to others that is undertaken with the purpose of generating a positive effect and outcome for another' and is the definition of kindness used throughout this book.
- *Your thoughts, ideas, assumptions and actions about leadership, kindness and their relationship are framed by models you've learned about in various ways.* You can change them by learning and practicing new models such as kind leadership.

Notes

1 https://greatergood.berkeley.edu/topic/empathy/definition. Downloaded on November 27, 2020.

2 D. Goleman. What Makes a Leader. In *On Leadership*. Harvard Business Review Press, 2011, pp. 3–21, p. 16.

3 Ibid.

4 www.danielgoleman.info/daniel-goleman-want-a-loyal-team-choose-kindness-over-toughness/ Downloaded November 26, 2020.

5 Thupten Jinpa, *A Fearless Heart: How the Courage to Be Compassionate Can Transform Our Lives*, as quoted from *The Book of Joy: Lasting Happiness in a Changing World*, Penguin, New York, 2016, p. 252.

6 https://dalailamacenter.org/heart-mind-challenge/compassionate-and-kind Downloaded October 3, 2020.

7 Thupten Jinpa, *A Fearless Heart*, 2016, p. 252.

8 In person interview with Cheryl Jensen, November 9, 2020.

9 Email interview with James H. Hanson, M.D. October 13, 2020.

10 In person interview with Deondra Wardelle, October 26, 2020.

11 Email interview with Dorota Jasielska, November 3, 2020.

12 In person interview with Jim Semple, October 12, 2020.

13 In person interview with Ann Howell, October 17, 2020.

14 In person interview with Michelle Jorgensen on November 5, 2020.

15 www.buffalo.edu/news/news-releases.host.html/content/shared/mgt/news/men-still-more-likely-than-women-perceived-leaders-study-finds.detail.html, Downloaded November 29, 2020.

16 Ibid.

17 Ibid.

18 In person interview with Amir Ghannad, October 19, 2020.

19 Excerpt from Colin Powell. *It Worked for Me*, Apple Books, 2012. https://books.apple.com/us/book/it-worked-for-me/id487138181

20 https://meridian-magazine.com/courageously-compassionate-a-conversation-with-jacinda-ardern/ Downloaded October 12, 2020.

Chapter 2

The Five Key Characteristics of a Kind Leader

Kindness is one of the qualities that differentiates a manager from a leader. The former gets the things done, where the latter builds an engaged team. Great leaders are not afraid to be kind.

Dorota Jasielska, Professor, researcher and author

Discussion: Kind Leadership Starts with You

I was talking with a friend of mine, Debbie Eison, who retired from her role as a human resources leader to start her own leadership and career coaching practice. Debbie told me about a discussion she had recently with a client who was working on developing their leadership skills. When Debbie asked the client what their experience with kindness in leadership was, they started to laugh! They told Debbie that in the organizations they had worked in, kindness in leadership wasn't something they had seen or experienced. In fact, they'd experienced just the opposite.

> The CEO's of those organizations were just terrible. They would walk right by you in the hall and not even look at you. They never seemed to know your name until they needed something. Then, for a minute, they knew exactly who you were. Once they got what they wanted, they

DOI: 10.4324/9781003141433-2

> totally forgot about you and never even acknowledged or thanked you … until the next time they needed something.

Debbie's client went on to say that the Vice Presidents and Directors weren't much better. What top leaders modeled seemed to set the tone for the rest of the leaders in the organization, and it certainly wasn't a kind one![1] Maybe you have experienced this in an organization you've worked in. I know that I certainly have.

As you learned in Chapter 1, kindness isn't just about thoughts and feelings. It's about action:

> *Kindness is an* action *(or set of actions), connecting a person's internal feelings of* empathy *and* compassion *to* others *that is undertaken with the purpose of generating a* positive *effect and outcome for another.*

Followers take their cues of how to act based on the actions of their leader, so whether the follower is a lower-level leader, or an entry-level team member, a leader's actions have far ranging effects. Since every person switches between wearing their Leader Hat and Follower Hat multiple times throughout the day, creating kinder leadership isn't about how *someone else* needs to act; it's about how *you* need to act and what *you* need to do.

Leaders' Actions Create Culture

A leader's actions, kind or unkind, don't just have an influence on individual followers at the moment they are taken. Those actions also create culture. Whether it's the culture of a company, the culture of a country or culture within a community group or family, a leader's actions have broad effects. Just like leadership, there are myriad definitions of, and books and articles written about, culture. For this book, the definition that will be used is also a very simple one:

Culture is the way things are expected and allowed to be done around here.

Whether the 'here' is a family unit, political party, or business, its culture – *the way things are expected and allowed to be done* – is a collection of *actions*, *reactions*, and also *non-actions* (all possible actions that weren't chosen). In the story told by Debbie's client above, employees felt unseen and uncared for. They felt that as people, they weren't important, only their output was. That feeling, part of the organization's culture, was created and reinforced each time a leader passed an employee in the hallway and chose not to say hello or greet the employee by name.

Many organizations have mission, vision and values statements that are supposed to represent their culture. An article from *Inc.* magazine lists the twenty most commonly used words found in value statements. The words are integrity, respect, innovation, teamwork, excellence, customer focus, trust, diversity, accountability, openness, quality, honesty, passion, safety, community, service, collaboration, responsibility, people and commitment.[2] Often, though, the words that are listed in the values statements don't match the actions taken by leaders. An organization that I worked for many years ago had a vision statement that focused on treating employees with respect. However, when the CEO came to town, they always held off-site meetings in fancy hotels. They didn't even visit the locations where the employees were working. The words in the values statement said one thing. The actions of the CEO said another. Employees didn't feel respected. In fact, they felt exactly the opposite – disrespected.

This happens even in organizations that don't have explicitly stated values, such as family units. To help see the gap between stated values and culture, and the relationship to leaders' actions, put on your Follower Hat and spend a day taking a close look at the way the people who lead you act. Pay attention to political leaders, business leaders and the leaders in your family unit. Do their actions match the words in the organization's value statement? You'll find an exercise to help you do that in this chapter's Practice Section (Figure 2.2) on page 32. (You can stop and do the exercise now or continue reading and do it at the end of this chapter.)

Because followers take their cues from the actions of leaders, a culture in which leaders act unkindly and disrespectfully – regardless of what the organization's values state – gives permission for everyone to act in disrespectful ways. When followers put on their Leader Hats, they will likely act in similar ways as their leaders because they have been socialized to act in the ways that are allowed and expected in their culture. Culture, unkind or kind, isn't just something that magically appears. It's something that is created action after action on a daily basis.

That's one of the biggest reasons why how leaders act is so important. Kind leadership isn't about words on a page or in mission, vision and values statements. It's about action. As you will see, each of The Five Key Characteristics of a Kind Leader start with action words and go on to describe the way leaders should act to both model kind leadership for others and to create a kind culture.

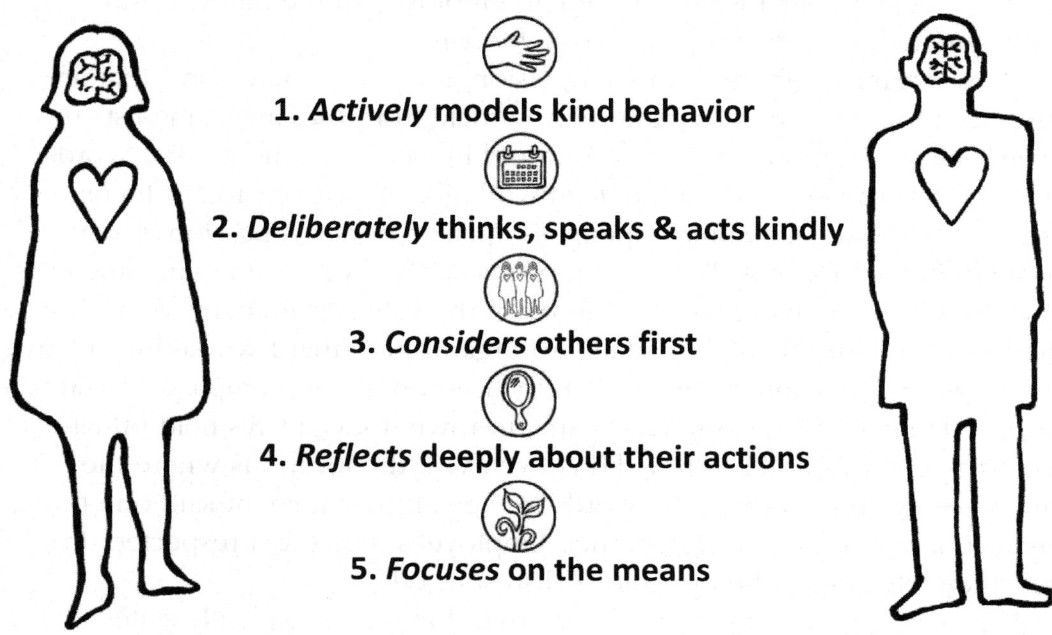

Figure 2.1 The Five Key Characteristics of Kind Leaders.

Kind Leaders Lead by Kind Example

The first two characteristics of Kind Leaders have to do with modeling kind behavior in a deliberate manner.

Key Characteristic 1: Kind Leaders *Actively Model* Kind Behavior

Kind behavior means a leader's ways of acting and reacting with empathy and compassion to create a positive outcome for followers. When I searched for the definition of the word behavior, I found that Oxford Languages, which provides Google's dictionary function defines it as "the way in which one acts or conducts oneself, especially toward others".[3] When a leader acts kindly toward others, it defines both what kind behaviors "look like" within that organization and also the expectations of how others should act.

Here's an example. At a Love and Kindness Project Foundation Country Directors' meeting just before the holidays, the team got together to brainstorm ideas for the yearly Holiday Kindness Tips. Everyone contributed great ideas, and one of the Country Directors volunteered to compile the ideas into a graphic that everyone could then share on their social media platforms. Before that person had a chance to create the graphic, one of the other Country Directors put their own together and shared it on their social media. As the Foundation's leader, I knew that how I behaved – the actions that I took – both toward the Director who shared too early and to the Director who had been expecting to create the graphic were extremely important. I needed to model kind behavior, not just because it was the right thing to do, but also because many of the Country Directors were new to their roles and were still learning about the culture of the Foundation.

Thinking about how both the Director who shared too early, and the Director who had been assigned to create the Holiday Tips might be feeling, I quickly reached out to each. First, I reached out to the Director who was assigned to create the graphic and apologized for not being clear enough in my communication that they would be the person creating the graphic! (After all, had I been clear enough, the mix-up wouldn't have happened in the first place.)

Second, I let the Director know that I still wanted her to go ahead and create the graphic as it would be valuable to the group and all of us would use it. Next, I contacted the Director who had shared too early, and apologized to her for not being clear enough in my communication. After I did that, guess what happened? She responded by saying that she had contacted the Director who had been assigned the work, apologized to her for not reading the communication carefully enough (having left the meeting a bit early, she hadn't heard that the other Director volunteered) and removed the post that she had shared too early. Because I, the leader, modeled the behavior of apologizing, the Country Director took my cue, and acted with the same kind behavior! Everyone makes mistakes and as the leader, it's my responsibility to model the behaviors that I want other leaders, and followers, in my organization to have when things inevitably go wrong. Knowing that that's the expectation and is the 'way things are allowed and expected to be done here' creates a kind culture as well.

Modeling kind behaviors isn't the only thing a leader needs to do. A leader also needs to define the specific behaviors that are allowed in their organization and that they expect to see (and those that aren't as well). As discussed above, it's not enough to say that your organization values treating people with respect. People throughout the organization need to know the specific behaviors associated with the value: saying hello to each other when passing in the hallway, not interrupting others while they are speaking and trying out ideas given by employees. Cheryl Jensen, the former CEO and President of Algonquin College, which has the organizational value of *Caring*, smiled and said hello to every person, student, staff and faculty, that she passed in her many walks through the campus each day. She stopped and talked with those who had questions and suggestions or just needed some of her time. By doing this, during her tenure as President, Cheryl actively modeled the value of *Caring* every single day.[4]

Kind Leaders actively choose kind behaviors to model how *others* should act. That includes the way they act, and the words they choose to use, because speaking is an action as well! As discussed in the Introduction (and as I'm sure you've experienced in watching the news on television), the words leaders choose to use are picked up and echoed throughout their organization. Those words create and become part of the culture as well. Actively modeling kind leadership is also about word choice and how those words are said. In Chapter 5 (Speak Kindly) and Chapter 6 (Act Kindly), you'll go more in depth on these topics.

Key Characteristic 2: Kind Leaders *Deliberately* Think, Speak and Act Kindly

I'm sure you have all heard the phrase 'random acts of kindness'. There is even a day set aside each year to celebrate those random acts. Here's the problem with 'random acts' when it comes to kind leadership. As I'm sure you know from wearing your Leader Hat, a leader's day can be very busy! Things that aren't deliberately planned may or may not happen. Since actively modeling kind behavior is such an important part of a leader's role, leaving it to chance – and hoping that it will randomly happen – isn't enough. As I so often say to my clients and the people that I'm coaching, "Hope isn't a strategy". Defining what kind behaviors are expected and actively modeling kindness to create a kind culture is something that Kind Leaders approach deliberately.

During the COVID-19 pandemic, I had the opportunity (and honor) to work with Petrina McGrath, a healthcare leader in Saskatchewan, Canada. Petrina's Quality and Safety team had the unbelievably important responsibility of keeping healthcare workers and patients safe during the pandemic. To do this, Petrina's team had to work with many departments within the provinces' healthcare authority and with front-line staff directly caring for patients. A difficult and stressful time for all. As fall turned to winter, COVID-19 cases started to surge, and Petrina saw that her extremely dedicated team was tired and stressed. To guide the team's weekly scheduled reflection time, Petrina sent an email challenging people to deliberately plan to be kind to themselves. Here is part of that email:

> Good Morning Everyone,
>
> And Thank you! Thank You for the incredible work each of you and your teams have done this week. This is hard work, the hardest of our careers. I am grateful every day that you are part of my team, and I know that we can get through any obstacle or challenge when you have great people, with diverse skills, talents and perspectives aligned and rowing in the same direction focused on a shared purpose.
>
> Once again, I am asking you to prioritize your reflection practice, create a space to step up on the balcony and observe yourself over the last week on the dance floor. If you can't do it at 8:00 am that is okay, just commit to finding thirty minutes in the next twenty-four hours for yourself.
>
> **Reflection – Looking back**
>
> Reflect on the last week and write down:
>
> - What did you notice?
> - What were you able to accomplish? What are you proud of over this last week?
> - What did you learn about yourself? Your team? From others around you?
> - Where did you feel triggered or challenged? What was going on for you? (Time of day, amount of sleep, food you ate or didn't eat, particular person, event)
>
> **Plan – Looking forward – Your challenge in the week ahead**
>
> How will you build into your day one thing that is about BEING KIND TO YOURSELF and acknowledging OTHERS?

- What is one thing that will be about your self-care (your oxygen mask)? What is your plan? How will you set up a daily check/study and adjust/adopt? What help do you need to follow through? Who can be your accountability partners?
- How will you notice and acknowledge others this week? Please keep it simple!

> Please send me your reflections. A photo if you wrote it on paper (no need to retype), by email if you are doing it that way or via text.[5]

As you can see, Petrina didn't leave helping her team be deliberate about kindness to chance. She planned it into their regular reflection practice. By challenging her team and asking them to deliberately plan their actions, Petrina both modeled the kind behavior and the deliberate attention to kindness she expects.

Being deliberate about thinking, speaking and acting kindly isn't just necessary for business leaders. It's important for leading at home, in the community and for political leaders as well. In an article in *Meridian* magazine, New Zealand Prime Minister Jacinda Ardern addresses the importance of being deliberate:

> "When I first came into politics, one of the criticisms I received was that I was not aggressive enough, not assertive enough", Ardern admits. She explains that a certain brutality and an ability to "claim 'scalps'", is expected of politicians. But Ardern did not buy into this. Instead, she recognised what few politicians seemed to notice, which is that "those aren't necessarily the traits that the public are looking for". She describes, then, making "a very deliberate decision" not to compromise her intuitive leadership style in order to be politically successful.[6]

For leaders, actively modeling kind behavior and creating a kind culture takes deliberate effort. The thoughts a leader thinks, the words they choose to use (and those they don't) and the actions and reactions they take need to be deliberately kind. Random acts won't lead to a kinder culture and create the new model for leadership so desperately needed.

Kind Leaders Are 'People' (Not 'Things') Oriented

The next two characteristics of Kind Leaders are focused on people, both on followers and on the leader themself.

Key Characteristic 3: Kind Leaders *Consider* Others First

Think about the traditional leaders you know. Whether politically or in business settings, what are most leaders focused on? A few of the first answers that come to mind are: business growth, financial results (both top and bottom-line), beating the competition and winning more market-share. All of those are 'things'. Kind Leaders aren't focused on 'things', they are focused on people. And per the definition of kindness being used, they are focused on considering how their actions can generate positive effects and outcomes for others. Because organizations (and countries, communities and families) are made up of people, and without other people to lead, leaders wouldn't actually be leaders, I'm always surprised when leaders consider 'things' first.

The CEOs described by Debbie Eison's client who walked down their organization's hallways without acknowledging or greeting passing employees, weren't considering other's first. Perhaps they were deep in thought about the next acquisition or merger, or about how to fend off a challenge from a competitor with an innovative new product, but what they didn't consider was the negative effect their actions had on the people they were leading; the very people who were needed to do the work necessary to solve the organization's problems and help it reach its goals.

Kind Leaders deliberately consider the needs of others first. When choosing how to act and react in day-to-day interactions such as business meetings and in making business decisions, especially tough ones that might have negative effects. Craig Delmage, an IT manager, sent me a great example of how a leader puts others first. He explained that in the regularly scheduled one-on-one meetings he has with his team members, instead of starting with his own agenda of what he wants to talk about, he always lets the team member go first. They can discuss whatever is on their mind, business or personal. After the team member has finished, Craig asks about whether he's made any decisions that have negatively affected the team member, or that they haven't agreed with. Only if there is time left after discussing the team member's items will Craig bring up what he wishes to cover. Craig says that, "by letting them go first, it sends a powerful signal that what they have to say is important to me. I may prompt them with some initial open-ended questions such as 'how are things going for you?' or 'how is your new baby?' or 'are you managing work/life balance ok?'" Craig has found that considering others first has had great benefits and says that, "Overall, I find that this approach works very well, and I have become closer to my team members – both on a work and personal front, as a result".[7]

Gretchen Dieter, a payroll leader, has more to add about one-on-one's and considering others first. Gretchen says that if an emergency comes up and there is a need to reschedule, she always lets the employee know why. She also makes sure to put the new meeting time on the same day or the next one. As Gretchen says, "I don't want to 'pretend' to be engaged and I want to give them the attention they deserve. If you reschedule, it must be done right away, or you leave the employee thinking they are unimportant".[8] In Chapter 3 (How We Get There Is as Important as Where We Are Going), you will learn more about how considering others first and getting to know your employees as people, creates a kind culture in which leaders and followers trust each other.

Although 'leading' is often associated with being first (think leading troops into battle, the President speaking first in a political forum, company leaders sitting at the front at the annual general meeting), Kind Leaders consider the needs of the people they lead first. As Amir Ghannad, author of *The Transformative Leader* said when I interviewed him,

> Kindness is practicing empathy in understanding others' needs and desires, and taking action based on that! It's not "do unto others as you would like to have done unto you", but "do unto others as they would like to be done to them".[9]

Even though employees are often spoken of in 'non-human' terms: resources or human 'capital', for example, people are never 'things' or 'dollar' amounts. They are human beings, with individual wants and needs that Kind Leaders need to consider first.

Key Characteristic 4: Kind Leaders *Reflect* Deeply about Their Actions

Everyone makes mistakes. It's a condition of being human. And since leaders are human, it's inevitable that they will make mistakes as well. Getting everything done that needs to be done, as well as actively and deliberately modeling kindness, and considering what others need first isn't easy to do. That's why, Kind Leaders spend time reflecting deeply about their actions.

Earlier in this chapter, you saw how healthcare leader Petrina McGrath deliberately builds weekly reflection time into her team's schedule. She doesn't just ask each of her team members to reflect though. Petrina has an extremely strong daily reflection process that helps her 'see' when she isn't acting in the way she wants to and isn't modeling the behaviors she wants her team members to have. In the fall of 2020, in advance of the expected cold weather COVID-19 surge, Petrina decided to move her three times a week team huddle to a daily one. Petrina asked if I, as her coach, could attend the daily huddles to give her feedback on her leadership. Petrina both wanted the feedback, and for her team to see the coaching process she was going through.

During the second week of the new daily huddle process, I kept getting text messages from Petrina before the huddle started that said things like, "I have a conflict this morning so can't attend my huddle. I'm assigning one of the team members, Patti, to lead it".[10] Finally, on Friday, when I received yet another text message from Petrina about a conflict that would cause her to miss huddle, I asked Petrina how many times she, the leader, had attended huddle during the week. She responded that it would only be two out of five times. When I asked Petrina if she thought that was the right amount for her to attend, she responded that it wasn't. Later, when I logged on remotely to the huddle, I was surprised to see Petrina there, ready to lead. I was even more surprised, when at the end of the huddle, Petrina read the string of text messages that we had sent to each other to her team members. Petrina then apologized for not actively modeling the behavior of considering their needs first and deliberately clearing her calendar and turning down other meetings scheduled during huddle time.[11] In being open about her own shortcomings and apologizing for her mistakes, Petrina used her ability to reflect deeply on her own actions to actively model the kind of behavior she expected from her team members. And just as importantly, Petrina was able to see where her behavior didn't match her expectations and change her actions so that it did. Petrina has attended and led her own huddles every day since!

As human beings, no one is perfect. No one, including leaders, acts and reacts as they would like to in all situations at all times. Regularly taking the time to deeply reflect is extremely important, because it's the way that Kind Leaders make the gaps in how they wanted to act – and how they actually acted – visible. Then they can make a deliberate plan to act differently next time.

Kind Leaders Pay Attention to 'How We Get There' Not Just 'Where We Are Going'

The last characteristic of Kind Leaders is that they pay just as much attention to how outcomes and results are achieved as to the outcomes and results themselves.

Key Characteristic 5: Kind Leaders *Focus* on the Means

Many leadership models that people are familiar with frame the most important characteristic of a leader as 'results-oriented'. Some of you may even have that term on your resume or LinkedIn profile! Whether those results are winning a war, producing record returns for shareholders, top- and bottom-line quarterly financial results or a balanced budget, many leaders are focused *first* on results, or what I call 'the ends'. The 'ends' are what happens *after* the work is done, whether that work is fighting a war, selling products and services to customers, or managing costs. I'm sure that you can add many other 'ends' that leaders you know are accountable for. Take a close look at the list, and one of the things you'll notice is that most of those 'ends' are 'things'.

As you've seen throughout this chapter, Kind Leaders aren't focused on 'things' first. They're focused on the people whose work produces the 'things'. And they are focused on *how* those 'things' are created, the 'means'. Because no matter what system or process the 'ends', or results, are created by, the common denominator that ties them all together is *people*. People create the computer programs and then program the robots in manufacturing plants. People interact with technology to book hotel rooms and flights. People answer customers' questions in health insurance call centers. Whatever 'ends' are produced by a company, people are involved. If the people who do the work to create the results aren't treated kindly, they won't be happy and engaged in the work that they are doing and the desired results, the 'ends', may not be achieved.

Grace Bourke, a process improvement practitioner, told me the following story that illustrates this perfectly. Shortly after starting a new job, Grace's manager came to her and said that he had been told to fire her. The results (ends) she was producing just weren't as expected. Instead of firing Grace, however, her manager asked if Grace could tell him what was going on. Grace explained that the onboarding and education she received wasn't adequate for her to be able to do the job as required. Grace and her manager then worked together to create a plan for Grace to build a reference guide with answers to questions that would help Grace do her job more effectively. Not only did the reference guide help Grace, it became a training document used throughout the company around the world. Grace stayed with the company for nine years, traveling, teaching and helping others throughout the organization.[12] Unlike the leaders in Debbie Eison's story, who cared only about their employee's output (the 'ends') and didn't pay any attention otherwise, Grace's leader cared about helping Grace be successful in her new role. By focusing on the 'means' he was able to ensure a great result as well!

Kind Leaders understand that by focusing on the means they will create both a better, kinder culture for the people who follow them (an important organizational 'end' in itself) which will, in turn, create better business results as well. You'll learn more about how that works in Chapter 3.

Keep the Five Key Characteristics in Mind

Throughout the rest of the book, you'll see the Kind Leader Characteristic Icons (the symbols located at the top left of the start of each of the Key Characteristics) in a variety of places. When you see those icons, stop and think about that Key Characteristic and its role in the discussion taking place.

Practice: Practical Exercises to Use to Turn Your Thoughts into Action

Now that you've read all about the Five Key Characteristics, it's time to apply that theory to your own experience. Remember, since everyone switches between wearing their Leader and Follower Hats, kind leadership isn't about someone else, it's about you! If you haven't done so already, please take the time now to complete the two exercises below.

Exercise 1: How Do Organizational Values and Leadership Behaviors Match?

Put on your Follower Hat and pay attention to political leaders, business leaders and the leaders in your family. Do their actions match the words in their value statements?

Do the actions leaders take match the organizational values stated? List your organization's written values (country, work, home). Next list leaders' actions. Do they match the written values?		
Organizational Values	**Leaders Actions**	**Values match? Why or why not?**
Country:		
Work:		
Home:		

Figure 2.2 Do your organization's values and leaders' actions match?

Exercise 2: How Do the Five Key Characteristics Apply to You?

Wearing your Leader Hat, take some time to thoughtfully evaluate yourself on the Five Key Characteristics. How do you exhibit each characteristic? When do you exhibit it? When don't you? If you'd like, you can ask others for their input as well.

How do you exhibit The Five Key Characteristics of a Kind Leader? Put on your Leader Hat and 'look closely' at yourself. Write down examples of how & Five Key Characteristics		
Kind Leader Key Characteristic	**How do I Exhibit the Characteristic?**	**When do I Exhibit It?**
Actively models kind		
Deliberately thinks, speaks and acts kindly		
Considers others first		
Reflects deeply about their actions		
Focuses on the means		

Figure 2.3 How do you currently exhibit The Five Key Kind Leader characteristics?

Reflection: What Would You Do? Kind Leader Practice Scenarios

Now that you've had the opportunity to read the ideas and theory presented in the Discussion section and do the Practice exercises, it's time to put on your Leader Hat, reflect on what you've learned and proactively plan how to apply those learnings.

Let's go back to the stories of Kay'La Janson and Kevin Landrell and see how each of them are doing in their new roles.

Do As I 'Say' and *As I Do!*

Scenario 1: Kay'La's Story: What Does Respect Look Like?

A month had passed since Kay'La Janson's first day at Codstom Industries. It had been a whirlwind of activity. Meetings with angry customers. Meetings with unhappy suppliers. And meetings with discouraged, despondent, disgruntled employees. There didn't seem to be one single happy person associated with Codstom. Kay'La checked her watch. It was eight-fifty-five in the morning. Only five more minutes until her daily Senior Leadership Check-In meeting. When Kay'La took over as CEO, the executive team was shocked to find out that she expected to meet with them every day. Previously, all they'd had was a day-long Month-in-Review meeting to go over the previous month's results. If deemed necessary, ad-hoc meetings were added during the month, but mostly, the executives, like the other lower-level leaders, managers and supervisors communicated with each other by email, even if their offices were right next door!

As Kay'La updated the date on the Senior Leadership Daily Check-In whiteboard, the execs came in and took their regular seats at the conference table. Kay'La turned and cheerfully said, "Good morning everyone! Great to see you as usual. Lots to look forward to today! Let's get started with reviewing how everyone's teams are doing". It had taken a while to get the execs to even understand why she wanted to know how their teams were doing – the problems they were having, how their morale was, and anything they needed help with – not just about the previous day's business results! But in the past few days, Kay'La could see that they seemed to be catching on. Most of the execs were now prepared with the information they were expected to provide each morning, and they were even starting to ask each other questions … and offer helpful suggestions! Everyone that is except for Anusha Patel, the Vice President of Finance.

Today, as usual, Anusha was five minutes late. And throughout the Check-In, she kept checking her smart watch, smart-phone and computer. Sometimes Anusha even stepped out briefly to take a call. "What I'm seeing from Anusha just doesn't go with our value of 'Being Respectful'", Kay'La thought to herself. "I'm going to have to…"

Now It's Your Turn to Reflect and Apply

Put on your Leader Hat and think about how you would approach Anusha and what you would do. Which of the Key Characteristics would you focus on? Are there other actions you'd take for the rest of the organization? What reflections might you have? Write your ideas here:

Scenario 2: Kevin's Story: "All's Well That 'Ends' Well"?

Kevin Landrell's first month as a supervisor had passed by in a flash! "I always wondered what the supervisors *really* did", Kevin laughed to himself! "Well, now I know!" Truth is, being a supervisor – and a kind one – was harder than Kevin thought it was going to be. He was constantly being pulled into meetings and assigned extra tasks by his boss, the assistant branch manager, Cindy Yang. And this week, during the branch's weekly Supervisor meeting, he'd been horrified and embarrassed to find out that his team wasn't performing up to standard. "We've got the worst results of any branch in our Area", Cindy had said. "If we don't get our scores up, I don't know what's going to happen … but I do know it's not going to be good for anyone. And, Kevin, you're a big part of the reason that we're all in trouble. Your team is bringing us all down".

Then she dropped a stack of papers onto the table in front of him. "Take a look at these. They're all terrible surveys for your team members. You'd better figure out what to do about them. And soon!"

After the meeting, Kevin thumbed through the stack of surveys. He noticed that most of the worst ones were for Jaden, the customer service rep who sat right beside Molly. Jaden was pretty new to the team. He'd only started with Codstom about a month before Kevin took over as supervisor. Kevin was surprised that Jaden's surveys weren't better. Jaden had a lot of previous customer service experience and the supervisor who had hired him had raved about his references. Jaden seemed to pick up on how to do the work quickly … Things just didn't add up. "I think I'm going to …".

Now It's Your Turn to Reflect and Apply

Put on your Leader Hat and think about what you would do about Jaden's poor surveys. Which of the Key Characteristics would help you decide what to do in this situation? Write about what you would do here:

Chapter 2 Kind-Points

- *Key Characteristic 1: Kind Leaders Actively Model Kind Behavior.* Behaviors are ways of acting toward others. When leaders act and react kindly, with empathy and compassion and the purpose of creating a positive outcome for others, followers take those cues as the ways they should act. The actions a leader takes creates organizational culture, kind or not.
- *Key Characteristic 2:* Kind Leaders *deliberately* think, speak and act kindly. Creating a kind culture is too important to be left to chance. Leaders need to 'plan' ways they are going to be model kind behavior deliberately.
- *Key Characteristic 3:* Kind Leaders *consider* others first. Although leaders are often thought of as being focused on 'things' like financial performance and results, Kind Leaders consider the effects of actions and decisions on people first. People should never be thought or treated 'things'.
- *Key Characteristic 4:* Kind Leaders *reflect* deeply about their actions. No one is perfect and everyone, including leaders, makes mistakes. Kind Leaders reflect often and deeply to see when they don't model the kind behaviors they planned to. The reflection process allows them to be more deliberate in future.
- *Key Characteristic 5:* Kind Leaders *focus* on the means. Kind Leaders aren't just 'results-oriented'. They focus on the means: creating a kind culture so that the people who do the work to create those results can flourish. Focusing on the means ensures great results for all.

Notes

1. Personal conversation with Debbie Eison on December 3, 2020.
2. www.inc.com/james-archer/20-words-you-can-drop-from-your-core-values-right-now.html Downloaded December 4, 2020.
3. https://languages.oup.com/google-dictionary-en/ Downloaded on December 5, 2020.
4. In person interview with Cheryl Jensen on November 9, 2020. I also witnessed this kind behavior many times between 2017 and 2019 while walking the halls with Cheryl!
5. Email from Petrina McGrath to her Safety and Quality team on December 4, 2020.
6. https://meridian-magazine.com/courageously-compassionate-a-conversation-with-jacinda-ardern/ Downloaded October 12, 2020.
7. Personal email from Craig Delmage, IT Manager, on August 31, 2020.
8. Personal email from Gretchen Dieter, Payroll Leader, on August 31, 2020.
9. In person interview with Amir Ghannad, October 20, 2020.
10. From personal text message string from Petrina McGrath on October 16, 2020.
11. From personal interaction and text message with Petrina McGrath on October 16, 2020 and October 17, 2020.
12. Interview with Grace Bourke on October 12, 2020.

Chapter 3

Why *How We Get There* Is as Important as Where We Are Going

Trust and kindness are cousins. If there is a trust deficit, people will hold back.

Jim Semple, manufacturing leader

Discussion: The *Kind* of Culture You Have Depends on the *Kind* of Leader You Are

One of the things I say most often when coaching leaders is 'how we get there is as important as where we are going'. That's because, although traditional models of leadership focus primarily on 'ends' and results (where we are going), Kind Leaders need to focus on the 'means' (the way we get there) instead. As you'll see in this chapter, unkind leadership leads to an unkind culture of fear, which has a negative effect on followers. Kind leadership produces a kind culture in which followers trust that their leaders don't just have the 'ends' in mind but have their followers' best interests at heart.

As you discovered in Chapter 2, the actions leaders take don't just provide a model of behavior for individual followers. More broadly, those actions create culture: *the way things are expected and allowed to be done around here*. Wherever that 'here' happens to be, country, state, city,

DOI: 10.4324/9781003141433-3

business, non-profit or family unit, *how* its leaders choose to act, react (and how not to act and react as well) impacts the entire system and everyone in it. And the impacts don't just stop within the organization; they spill over to other areas as well.

I had a great aha-moment about this when talking with business owner and former Human Resources leader, Deondra Wardelle. During her Kind Leader interview, Deondra and I discussed the broad and far-reaching effects of leaders' actions on culture. "It's like that old cartoon that used to be so popular", I said. "You know the one where the boss yells at the supervisor, the supervisor yells at the worker, the worker goes home and yells at their spouse, the spouse then yells at the child and the child kicks the dog ...?" "Yes", Deondra said.

> I'm familiar with that one. But you know, it doesn't just stop there. The kid then goes to school and bullies other kids. And then they grow up, they get a job, go to work, and yell at the people who work for them. And the whole cycle starts all over again.[1]

Because all organizations are made up of people, and people belong to multiple different organizations (they're citizens of a country, members of community groups like sports teams and social clubs and members of nuclear and extended families), the behaviors that their leaders model and

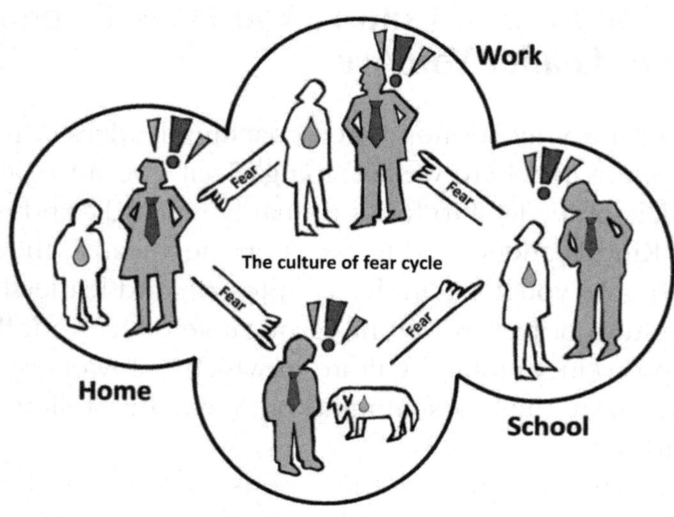

Figure 3.1 Unkind leaders spread fear across organizations and in a vicious circle.

that are expected and allowed in one organization, can be transferred easily to another. Perhaps the parent who shouts at the umpire at their child's little league baseball game has learned that behavior by seeing it modeled by the leaders in their workplace. Or the employee who says derogatory things about colleagues who have immigrated from other countries is acting out one of the behaviors that political leaders they follow model.[2] And if that isn't enough, because every person switches between their Follower and Leader Hats constantly, behaviors learned as a follower in one organization's unkind culture can be spread within another organization when that same person puts on their Leader Hat.

Leaders need to be conscious that the culture their actions create isn't just going to affect their followers, but everyone else their followers interact with.

Leaders Who Focus on the Ends Only Can Create a Culture of Fear

Many years ago I worked in an extremely results-focused, 'ends'-oriented company. Leadership's favorite phrase was 'the number is the number' and it was repeated over and over again. Even though the company's mission, vision and values statements focused on working together cooperatively and treating every individual with respect, we all knew that the end result, 'the number' was the only thing that really mattered. The number of customer calls taken, the number of minutes and seconds each of those calls took, the office's national ranking in the organization and, most importantly, the dollar number of the quarterly financial results. During employees' weekly one-on-ones, the first (and only thing) discussed were their 'numbers'. Poor performance on call time metrics or customer satisfaction survey scores would result in an unpleasant 'talking to' or remedial retraining. It's not surprising that employees felt that they weren't valued for who they were as people, and that they were simply just 'a number'. Not only did employees dread their weekly one-on-one's, they actually feared them.

KLC Stop & Think Point: People are never 'numbers'. Yet they're often referred to in numerical or non-human terms: head-'count', resources, human 'capital'. Put on your Leader Hat and think about what terms your organization uses. Are they human or not? What's the effect on your organization's culture?

I was thinking about this the other day as I was talking with Lili Boyanova, The Love and Kindness Project Foundation's Country Director who made the mistake of sending Holiday Tips out too early that you read about in Chapter 2. As we talked about what happened, Lili told me how meaningful it was that instead of focusing on the *outcome* of the mistake she made (the 'ends') I focused on the process that had resulted in the mistake happening (the 'means'). "Everybody makes mistakes", Lili said.

> In so many of the organizations that I've worked in, people don't want to admit that they've made a mistake. Or else they try to cover up their mistakes because they're afraid of what's going to happen. What their leader is going to say or do to them. Working in that kind of culture of fear is terrible. It can stop people from being their best and giving their best. And it can have long term negative results in other areas of their life.[3]

I'm sure you've heard many other stories of people who have worked in environments in which the unkind actions of leaders have created a culture of fear. Leaders who shout at or ridicule employees who have made an error, leaders who publicly point out an individual's poor performance on metrics during meetings, and leaders who make veiled threats about job losses if results don't improve dramatically.

As Lili said, when employees are afraid of the reactions they may get from unkind leaders, it prevents them from being their best and doing their best. From employees who are afraid to raise concerns about the safety of a new product or service, to those who have great ideas but are afraid to voice them for fear of ridicule, to those who fear losing their jobs if they disagree with a management decision or the way it is carried out, fear stops people from acting in ways that can prevent problems and create better products and services.

Fear also makes people stressed and unhappy. And those feelings of fear and stress spread from one environment to another. I'm sure you know people who bring the fear they feel at work home. People who can't sleep at night. People who spend all day Sunday worrying about what's to come on Monday. And as discussed above, people who take out their fear, anger and frustration by yelling at family members. The negative effect of unkind, ends-focused, fear-based culture doesn't just stay within an organization. It spreads out into social and family units as well, resulting in people who don't just work in fear, but live in fear.

Have you ever worked in an organization that had a culture of fear? Where you were afraid to make a mistake, voice your opinion or offer a perspective that was different from others'? Or perhaps you're currently living in a situation where a culture of fear in a wider social context has spilled over into your family life. To better understand the results of that culture of fear, put on your Follower Hat and think about how you and others have been negatively affected because of it. You'll find an exercise to help you do that in this chapter's Practice Section (Figure 3.3) on page 52. (You can stop and do the exercise now or continue reading and do it at the end of this chapter.)

Kindness and Fear Don't Go Together!

If you've spent most of your career working in an unkind, results-oriented, fear-based environment, I've got some good news for you. There is an alternative! In a *Forbes* article on workplace fear, career coach Liz Ryan says that,

> A fear-based workplace is a place where fear is the predominant energy. A healthy workplace is one where trust is the predominant energy. Trust and fear cannot co-exist in the same place. People who pretend they can co-exist are afraid to admit what their body knows: managerial fear overpowers trust every time.[4]

When ends-focused leaders treat followers unkindly, those followers feel like leaders care more about the results than they do about them. When leaders treat followers kindly, they don't feel fear. What they feel, instead is trust. They trust that their leaders don't just value them for the results they can produce, but care about them as people. Kind Leaders create a culture of trust, not by focusing on 'things' and end-results, but, as you'll see, by focusing on the means: *how we get there.*

Leaders Who Focus on the Means Can Create a Culture of Trust

Just like leadership and culture, a myriad of books and articles have been written both about the concept of trust, and about trust and leadership. According to the *Merriam-Webster* dictionary trust is a verb (an action word) that means "to rely on the truthfulness or accuracy of (believe in); to place confidence in (rely on a friend you can trust); and to hope or expect confidently".[5] Throughout this book, in relation to kind leadership, the definition of trust that will be used is:

Trust means that followers believe that leaders have their best interests at heart at all times.

To create a culture of trust, leaders need to focus on creating *conditions and an environment* where followers see that their needs are considered first, and not just as an afterthought, or not considered at all! As you saw in Chapter 2, instead of firing Grace without an explanation because she wasn't 'performing' well and delivering results, her manager helped Grace create a plan to make a tool that would allow her to do her job successfully. Grace's manager focused on the means – how we get there – so that Grace (and the organization) could get to 'where they were going'. By considering Grace's needs first, her manager built a culture of trust. A culture in which Grace stayed nine more years!

Thinking back to The Five Key Characteristics of a Kind Leader, you can see how they align perfectly with creating a culture of trust:

Key Characteristic 1: Kind Leaders *actively model* kind behavior. The actions Kind Leaders choose (and those they don't) are based on thoughts and feelings of empathy and compassion.

Key Characteristic 2: Kind Leaders *deliberately* think, speak and act kindly. The deliberate choices Kind Leaders make have the underlying purpose of creating positive outcomes for others.

Key Characteristic 3: Kind Leaders *consider* others first. Kind Leaders understand that each follower is a valuable human being who will learn, grow and contribute their best when treated kindly in a culture of trust.

Key Characteristic 4: Kind Leaders *reflect* deeply about their actions. No one is perfect, so Kind Leaders reflect deeply to see where their actions may have focused solely on the ends and created fear in their followers.

Key Characteristic 5: Kind Leaders *focus* on the means. Kind Leaders focus their time and energy on creating conditions – the means – that help their followers do their best and be their best so that the end results can be achieved kindly.

KLC Stop & Think Point: No leader is perfectly kind all the time. The leader whose favorite saying was 'the number is the number' also made sure all holidays were celebrated so everyone felt included. Put on your Leader Hat and think about how deliberate you are in focusing on the means before the ends.

In a kind culture of trust, when people know that leaders have their best interests at heart, they aren't afraid to step out of their comfort zone to try new things. When I asked Skip Steward, Chief Improvement Officer at Baptist Memorial Health Care Corporation, to tell me about a time when he had experienced kindness from someone who was leading him, Skip told me about working on yearly goals with his manager Dr. Paul DePriest. "When Dr. DePriest told me the goals he had set out for the year, they seemed so lofty that at first I didn't want to sign up for them. But Dr. DePriest was so kind and I had such a profound level of trust that he had my best interests at heart and believed that I could do it, I signed up for them. Because Dr. DePriest was so encouraging, and because he believed so strongly in me, I had the courage to do things I didn't think I would be able to".[6] Working in a culture of trust created by his leader, Skip wasn't afraid to try new things. In fact, knowing that Dr. DePriest had Skip's best interests at heart removed the fear and allowed for Skip's personal growth. Great for Skip and for the organization's results as well.

In a culture of trust, one of the biggest reasons followers feel safe enough to try new things is because they aren't afraid to admit mistakes. As Lili and I continued our conversation about the mistake she made sending out the Holiday Tips referenced above, Lili told me that because I (the leader of The Foundation) apologized to her and admitted that I had made a mistake, instead of feeling fearful, she felt comfortable in admitting her mistake, and confident in reaching out to apologize to the other Director. "No one is perfect", Lili said. "Sometimes I don't read things carefully and I act too quickly. Because I knew I wasn't going to be shamed, I wasn't afraid. I could just do the right thing and reach out. Instead of making me feel terrible, the whole experience has helped me to learn and grow".[7] Because I admitted my mistake and apologized, Lili wasn't afraid to admit hers. No one is perfect. Everyone makes mistakes. When leaders create a culture of trust, followers know that making a mistake isn't something to be feared, it's something to learn and grow from.

Have you had an experience where trusting that a leader had your best interests at heart helped you overcome fear to learn and grow? Put on your Follower Hat and think about the positive effects that experience had on you in different areas of your life. You'll find an exercise to help you do that in this chapter's Practice Section (Figure 3.4) on page 53. (You can stop and do the exercise now or continue reading and do it at the end of this chapter.)

Together, Trust and Kindness Can Lead to Greater Happiness

When Kind Leaders create a culture of trust, it doesn't just lead to less fear for followers. It can actually lead to greater happiness. Published in *Current Psychology* in 2018, Dorota Jasielska's study, "The moderating role of kindness on the relationship between trust and happiness" shows the effects of kindness on *situational trust* where "trust is defined as handing over control to another person".[8] In the study, university students participated in a trust game, answered questions about trust and acts of kindness and completed a happiness scale.

As you can see in Figure 3.2, the graph showing the study's findings, the higher the level of trust there was, the happier people were. You can also see that kind acts, in combination with higher levels of trust, led to even greater happiness. As Jasielska says, "Trust alone can be a predictor of happiness but it seems that kindness strengthens this effect, and without at least some prosocial activity, people will not derive much happiness from being trustful".[9] To turn trust into happiness, kind acts were the key.

These finding are particularly important and relevant to the discussion about the ability of Kind Leaders to create a culture of trust in two ways. The first is that leaders are in positions of situational trust. Followers are asked to hand over control of many things to leaders. When those leaders act kindly, not only will their followers develop trust in them, but followers will be happier as well! The second, as you saw earlier, is that the effects of a culture a follower experiences in one place can be easily transferred to another. Like the old cartoon where the leader yells at the employee at work and the employee goes home and yells at their spouse, and a vicious cycle of unkindness and fear is created, a virtuous cycle of

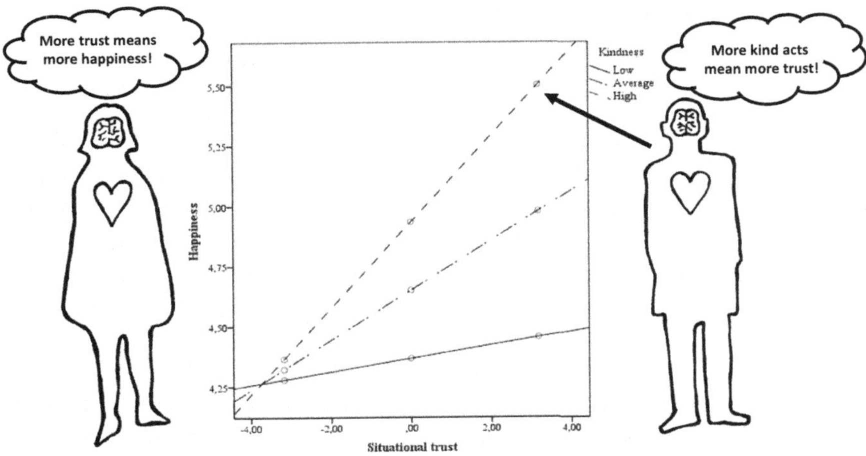

Figure 3.2 The effect of situational trust on happiness at different levels of kindness.[10]

kindness and trust can also be created. Followers who experience acts of kindness and cultures of trust will bring that model home to their families and communities. And it will be the model of leadership they use when they don their Leader Hats. Jasielska comes to this conclusion as well stating:

> If people had the chance to learn to trust others through practicing kindness, it could elevate their level of happiness and hence they might be willing to become involved in even more prosocial behaviors. This could have the potential of improving not only their subjective well-being, but also the social capital of countries.[11]

The 'kind' of culture you have really does depend on the 'kind' of leadership you have.

Why Kind Leadership and "Leaving People Alone" Don't Go Together

As I did the research for this book, I had many discussions with people, (both those in leadership and those in followership roles) about what trust meant from the *follower's* point of view. When they were wearing their Follower Hat, how did they know that their leader trusted them? The answer I got was almost the same every time: they knew their leader trusted them if their leader 'left them alone' to do their work. I've heard many other versions of this from the leadership side as well, such as "hire good people and get out of their way", attributed to leaders such as Lee Iacocca, Steve Jobs and Richard Branson.

As I reflected on this, I wondered if because, for leaders in most traditional organizations, only the 'ends' – the results – mattered, there would be no need to focus on the 'means'? That since it simply didn't matter 'how' the results were created, there was no need to spend time with the people who created the results. I also wondered if followers felt this way because, when working in a heavily results-focused environment, they were afraid: afraid that if their leader spent too much time with them, the leader might see the mistakes the followers were making and the struggles they were having, which could lead to a negative response or outcome.

For Kind Leaders, 'leaving people alone' isn't the way to create a culture of trust. Since Kind Leaders are focused on 'the means', spending time with followers is key. When leaders and followers spend time together, followers benefit from leaders deliberate acts of kindness. Glen Weppler, a higher education leader, told me the following story when I asked him to describe a time that he experienced kindness from someone who was leading him:

> When I started working in higher education, one of my early supervisors spent so much time with me. She always had time to take a call and answer my questions, and she would welcome me into her office, even if I showed up unannounced, to make sure that I was doing okay, and that I was learning and growing. She gave of her time so that she could understand what I was doing, what I needed and how she could help me develop.[12]

Glen's supervisor developed his capabilities and confidence by spending her time with him. Glen developed trust in his leader because he knew that she would be there for him when he needed her.

Deondra Wardelle, who you met earlier in this chapter, told me a story that stuck with her from a time early in her career. Deondra was working as a new store manager for a retail chain. She had to set up the floor for a significant store-wide sales promotion according to the chain's standards. She and the assistant store manager spent several days on the setup. They did their best but weren't confident in the result as the setup instructions were somewhat ambiguous. Deondra was even more worried because the regional manager had planned to visit the store to review the store set up for the sales promotion. When the regional manager arrived, Deondra's suspicions were confirmed. She hadn't set up the floor per the chain's requirements. The regional manager pointed out the differences, then rolled up her sleeves and showed Deondra how to set up the promotion properly. By the end of the day, the promotion setup looked great, and Deondra had developed trust – not fear – in her leader. Even though it was early in her career, as Deondra says:

> To this day, I still think about how the regional manager jumped in and didn't just tell me what to do, she was hands on yet didn't try to take over. She wanted to ensure I understood the specs in the document so that I would be more secure in doing future floor moves. There was another significant floor move the team and I completed prior to her next visit. When she arrived, I remember her eyes sweeping over every square inch of the store. Once she concluded her visual audit, she moved one rack half an inch, looked at me and said, 'Good job the store looks great'.

It still makes me feel great![13]

When leaders spend time helping their followers, fear is reduced, and trust is developed. An article in *Women's Health* magazine UK reports the following research results: "When we support others and do kind things for them, the activity in our amygdala (fear centres) goes down and sends a calming response to our body, meaning our cortisol (stress hormone) responds in a healthier way".[14] And, as you saw in Dr. Jasielska's research, kind acts, combined with higher levels of trust, lead to greater happiness. Kind Leaders know that 'leaving people alone to do their work' is 'ends'-focused and not the way to develop a kind culture of trust, no matter what followers might think. Spending time with people focusing on the 'means', how they get to the ends, is.

What about the 'Results' Though?

You may be thinking to yourself, "This 'means' stuff is all well and good, but don't leaders have to focus on the 'results' as well?" They do. In business, customers need to be satisfied with the company's products and services and the organization needs to remain financially viable. Non-profits need to serve the people who need their care, and governments need to function effectively to serve their constituents.

Although this book is not written to show you that the primary reason to be a kinder leader is to improve business results, better 'ends' do occur when people don't work in a culture of fear but instead work in a culture of trust. Leadership coach and consultant Ann Howell says, "It's important to remind people that kindness is not a weakness and it can co-exist with a profitable business … when there is no fear!"[15] In a *Harvard Business Review* article titled 'Why Compassion Is a Better Managerial Tactic than Toughness', author Emma Seppälä quotes Dr. James Doty, a director at Stanford University's Center for Compassion and Altruism Research and Education, on the effects of fear and lack of trust on work outcomes:

> Creating an environment where there is fear, anxiety and lack of trust makes people shut down. If people have fear and anxiety, we know from neuroscience that their threat response is engaged, their cognitive control is impacted. As a consequence, their productivity and creativity diminish.[16]

You saw that in both Grace and Lili's stories earlier in this chapter.

On the other hand, creating a culture of trust has been proven to produce better business results. In a blog on Great Place to Work's website linking the results of high-trust company cultures to success, the first measure listed is superior financial results, then higher stock market returns and higher operating income per employee, operating margin, growth rate and return on assets. Their conclusion: "Clearly, workplaces with a high-trust culture have a competitive bottom-line advantage in the marketplace".[17]

The 'results' of a culture of trust aren't just good for the bottom line. They are good for people too. Dr. Paul J. Zak, Harvard researcher and Founding Director of the Center for Neuroeconomics Studies at Claremont Graduate University has found, over two decades of research, that "compared with people at low-trust companies, people at high-trust companies report 74% less stress, 106% more energy at work, 50% higher productivity, 13% fewer sick days, 76% more engagement, 29% more satisfaction with their lives, and 40% less burnout".[18] And this isn't just good for business. As you saw earlier, the effects of culture (negative and positive) from one place transfers to others.

Amir Ghannad often talks about the work he did to lead a manufacturing plant turn-around from worst to best. As the plant's leader, he didn't just do it by focusing on manufacturing results. He aimed to create what he called the Cradle of Prosperity, in which he and his wife worked directly with the plant's employees to teach them about personal finance principles and other important life skills. As Amir says, "We didn't just focus on business results. We focused on helping people get better. Because when people were better, results improved. People think that kindness is counter to delivering results. But results go through the roof when a leader is kind".[19]

How Do You Get from a Culture of Fear to a Culture of Trust and Kindness?

It's clear that a culture of trust, created by kind leadership, in which followers believe that their leaders have their best interests at heart, is the best way to achieve all kinds of results. When leaders focus on the means, and help their followers learn, grow and gain confidence and happiness, there is no end to the benefits!

In the next three chapters, you'll see how leaders can move from creating a culture of fear to a culture of trust by thinking, speaking and acting kindly, and modeling those behaviors for their followers.

Now, if you haven't already, please take the time to complete the practice exercises in the following section.

Practice: Practical Exercises to Use to Turn Your Thoughts into Action

Is your culture primarily focused on the 'ends'? Or is it primarily focused on the 'means'? Is it one where people live in fear of their leader finding out they've made a mistake? Or is it one where people trust that those who lead them have their best interests at heart? As you saw, no leader is perfect and no culture is perfect. Take a close look at yours to understand where there is fear, and where there is trust and how you (and others) are affected in different areas of your life.

Exercise 1: Negative Effects of an Ends-Focused Culture on Fear

Think back to a time where you felt fearful and stressed. Put on your Follower Hat and describe the situation in detail. What actions did your leader take that made you feel that way? How did it affect you in that environment and in other areas of your life? What did you hold back? How did you treat others?

Negative effects of an ends-focused culture of fear Put your Follower Hat on and think about a time when you felt fearful about a leader's reaction. What did you think was going to happen to you? How did it affect your actions in that situation? How did it affect your actions in other parts of your life?	
Situation in which you felt fearful	**How that fear made me act and react**
Describe the situation:	At home:
What actions were you afraid your leader was going to take?	At work:
How did you feel?	In other situations:

Figure 3.3 Working and living in a culture of fear has many negative 'spill-over' effects.

Exercise 2: Positive Effects of a Means-Focused Culture on Trust

Keeping your Follower Hat on, remember a time where you felt confident, relaxed and that you could give your best and be your best. Describe the situation in detail. What actions did your leader take that made you feel that way? How did it affect you in that environment and in other areas of your life? How did it help you? How did you treat others?

Positive effects of a means-focused culture of trust Keep your Follower Hat on and describe a time when you had the courage to try something new because of the trust you had in your leader. What did the leader do? How did it make you feel? What effects did it have on you longer term?	
Situation in which you felt encouraged to try something new	**How did those feelings of trust affect you?**
What new thing did you try?	At home:
What actions did your leader take to encourage you?	At work:
How did you feel?	In other situations:

Figure 3.4 Working and living in a culture of trust has positive 'spill-over' effects too.

Reflection: What Would You Do? Kind Leader Practice Scenarios

Now that you've had the opportunity to read the ideas and theory presented in the Discussion section and do the Practice exercises, it's time to reflect on what you've learned and proactively plan how to apply those learnings.

Time to check in on Kay'La Janson and Kevin Landrell and see how each of them are doing.

Trust Comes from Spending Time Together

Scenario 1: Kay'La's Story: What Are You Afraid of? And Why?

Anusha arrived a few minutes early for her meeting with Kay'La. Anderson ushered Anusha into Kay'la's empty office and got her settled at the round table that Kayla had ordered on her first day. There was always a small vase of flowers on the table and Kay'La refreshed it each week. As Anusha waited for Kay'La to arrive, she thought to herself,

> It's so unusual to be asked to have a one-on-one with the CEO. I must really be in big trouble. Business results are inching their way and up I can't think of anything I've done that could be so terrible. I hope I'm not going to get fired … .

Nervously, Anusha checked the time on her smartphone again.

Exactly at one o'clock, Kay'La walked into the room carrying two cups. As she sat down beside Anusha at the small table, Kay'La said, "I was down in the cafeteria talking with some of our servers, and I brought you this cup of tea. Hope you like it. I notice that you often have tea during our Daily Check-in". Anusha was surprised. This certainly wasn't what she had expected. "Thank you", she said, as she quickly glanced down at her smartphone. "Do you have another meeting soon?" Kay'La asked. "No", answered Anusha. "I cleared my calendar when I heard you wanted to see me. Why do you ask?" "Because you just checked your smartphone", Kay'La responded. "In fact, that's one of the reasons I asked you to meet me today. I notice that when we're in our Daily Check-in, you frequently check your phone and other devices. I wonder if you've noticed that and if there's something pressing at that time that makes it hard for you to give the meeting your full attention?"

Anusha paused for a moment. She wondered if she should tell the truth. Should she trust Kay'La? She had so much fear left-over from working with the former CEO. But Kay'La seemed different. After all, Kay'La had taken the time to invite her for this one-on-one, and she remembered that Anusha drank tea, rather than coffee. Anusha quickly glanced down at her phone one more time, and then said,

> I hope you're not going to be too angry with me for telling you this. The former CEO put so much pressure on me, especially in the last few months he was here, when results were sinking as quickly as the Titanic, that I've been overwhelmed with stress. And when I'm over-stressed, one of the things that I do is check my phone. It's a nervous habit I'm trying to break, but obviously it's not working. Every morning, I'm so worried about what might happen at Daily Check-in if the results have taken a dip that I guess my nervous habit is becoming noticeable to others. Including you!
>
> Kay'La took a sip of her coffee, looked thoughtfully at Anusha and…

Now It's Your Turn to Reflect and Apply

Put on your Leader Hat and think about what you would do in this situation. How could you help Anusha get over her fear and start to have her trust you? What other actions would you take on an organizational level? What questions might you be asking yourself and others? Write your ideas here:

Scenario 2: Kevin's Story: 'Seeing Is Believing ... and Trusting!'

Kevin and Jaden walked down the hall toward the conference room together. It was the same conference room that Kevin and the rest of the supervisors had been in when Cindy Yang had chewed him out. "I sure hope that this meeting isn't going to leave either Jaden or I feeling the way I felt after that meeting", Kevin thought to himself. As they sat down, Kevin noticed that Jaden was sweating profusely, and shaking a little bit. "Hey, Jaden", Kevin said. "Are you alright? You look really worried to me. Everything is going to be okay. I just have a few questions and want to have an honest discussion with you. I was a customer service rep here myself for a long time, and I know how hard it can be".

Jaden looked at Kevin and before Kevin could say anything else, Jaden started off on a long tirade. Kevin could hear the frustration in Jaden's voice.

> I'm so disappointed. When I interviewed for this job everyone told me how much training and support there would be in the beginning. That I'd get two weeks of classroom training, two weeks of on-the-job training, and then a buddy that would sit beside me to mentor me. Then I got here. And I guess because the company wasn't doing so well financially, the two weeks of training in class was cut to one, and I was just thrown onto the floor. Sink or swim. And Molly, who's supposed to be my mentor, just makes fun of me when I don't know things. She says, "Didn't you learn that in training? It's so basic. You must not have been paying attention". Now I've got a pile of bad surveys and no one's said anything about what's going to happen. My partner is out of work, and if I lose my job, I don't know what we're going to do. I'm just constantly living in fear. At work, and at home.

Jaden stopped talking and put his head in his hands. That's when Kevin…

Now It's Your Turn to Reflect and Apply

Put on your Leader Hat. What would you do to help Jaden? What would you do on a wider organizational level? How would you approach Cindy Yang with what you've found? Write about what you would do here:

Chapter 3 Kind-Points

- *When leaders focus only on the ends a culture of fear can be created.* Focusing on the 'ends' means focusing on 'things' and 'results', without regard for how those results are produced, and the people who produce them. This can create a culture of fear in which people hide mistakes and feel like they are just a 'number'. This type of culture can prevent people from doing their best and being their best.
- *Cultures of fear spread easily and replicate themselves in a vicious circle.* Because people switch often between wearing their Leader Hat and their Follower Hat, someone who works in a culture of fear as a follower, may be a leader elsewhere in their life and replicate the ends-focused behaviors their leaders have modeled. In this way, a culture of fear can spread and replicate.
- *Leaders who focus on the means can create a culture of trust.* The definition of trust that will be used throughout this book is: *Trust means that followers believe that leaders have their best interests at heart at all times.* Leaders who display The Five Key Characteristics of a Kind Leader can create a culture of trust that is focused not on the ends, but on the 'means', the way in which the 'results' are created.
- *Why Kind Leadership and "leaving people alone" don't go together.* Since trust is built by seeing leaders deliberately model kind acts, and by leaders helping followers to learn, grow and be successful in their work, 'leaving people' alone to struggle and fail doesn't work. Spending time focused on the means and kindly helping people does!
- *Kind Leadership does have better 'results'.* Better financial and organizational 'ends' do occur when people work in a culture of trust and not a culture of fear. Additionally, the 'results' are also better for people's well-being, happiness and for their lives and society as a whole.

Notes

1. Personal interview with Deondra Wardelle on October 26, 2020.
2. Look carefully at Figure 3.0 and compare it to Figure 1.0: Kindness connects leaders to followers through positive action on page 8. Notice that these figures are the opposite of each other.
3. Personal conversation with Lili Boyanova on December 9, 2020.
4. www.forbes.com/sites/lizryan/2017/03/07/ten-unmistakable-signs-of-a-fear-based-workplace/?sh=24778d5f1e26 Downloaded on December 13, 2020.
5. www.merriam-webster.com/dictionary/trust Downloaded on December 12, 2020.
6. Personal interview with Skip Steward on Monday, October 12, 2020.
7. Personal conversation with Lili Boyanova on December 9, 2020.
8. D. Jasielska, The Moderating Role of Kindness on the Relation Between Trust and Happiness. *Current Psychology* 39 (2020): 2065–2073. https://doi.org/10.1007/s12144-018-9886-7
9. Ibid.
10. Graph from D. Jasielska. Ibid.
11. Ibid.
12. Personal interview with Glen Weppler on October 5, 2020.
13. Personal interview Deondra Wardelle on October 26, 2020.
14. www.womenshealthmag.com/uk/health/mental-health/a34600669/physical-benefits-of-kindness/ Downloaded November 16, 2020.
15. Personal interview with Ann Howell on October 19, 2020.
16. https://hbr.org/2015/05/why-compassion-is-a-better-managerial-tactic-than-toughness Downloaded December 14, 2020.
17. www.greatplacetowork.com/resources/blog/8-ways-great-company-culture-drives-business-success Downloaded December 13, 2020.
18. www.inc.com/marissa-levin/harvard-neuroscience-research-reveals-8-ways-to-build-a-culture-of-trust.html Downloaded December 13, 2020.
19. Personal interview with Amir Ghannad on October 19, 2020.

Chapter 4

Think Kindly

Kind Leaders Assume Positive Intent

Your thoughts create the words you speak and influence your actions.
Karyn Ross

Discussion: Kind Leadership Takes Practice

Now that you've learned about The Five Key Characteristics of a Kind Leader and seen that kind leadership can create a culture of trust instead of a culture of fear, it's time to get down to the nitty-gritty, the 'how' of kind leadership. What are the things that leaders need to do, on a daily basis, to deliberately model kindness? What are the specific ongoing kind leadership practices that will create that culture of trust where followers believe their leaders have their best interests at heart?

In the next three chapters, you'll learn about the *Three Key Kind Leader Practices: Think Kindly, Speak Kindly and Act Kindly*. Each Key Practice will have its own chapter, however, as you will see, all three are tied together, interconnected and influence one another. As well as understanding them from a theoretical perspective, you'll also learn how each of them is a *practice*. That means they're not just things to think about as an abstract, conceptual model, but have specific behaviors attached to each one. In the Discussion section of each chapter, you'll be introduced to the specific behaviors and the theory around them. In the Practice section, the exercises you'll be given

DOI: 10.4324/9781003141433-4

The Three Key Kind Leader Practices and Behaviors

Think Kindly Behaviors
- Always assume positive intent
- Check your thoughts frequently
- Consciously change unkind thoughts to kind ones

Speak Kindly Behaviors
- Choose your words kindly
- Use a kind tone of voice
- If it's not kind, don't say it!

Act Kindly Behaviors
- Check in with people, not on them
- Listen with open eyes, open ears, open mind and an open heart
- Recognize others

Figure 4.1 The Three Key Kind Leader practices.

to do to will help you use the behaviors in a variety of leadership situations at work, at home and in the community. Learning and becoming competent and confident with any type of new behavior takes concerted effort, so I encourage you to take your practice seriously! And practice daily. As I always say, *human beings learn by doing*, so the more you practice the behaviors the more comfortable you'll feel, and the easier they will get.

Thinking Kindly Is the First of Three Key Kind Leader Practices

The Three Key Kind Leader Practices flow from one another. You can start your practice with any of them, but for this book I'm going to start with the Think Kindly Practice. That's because unlike speaking and acting, where you hear the words you say, and see the actions that you take, the thoughts that you think aren't as easily visible. Sometimes you may be very conscious of your thoughts and other times, you may not be. Becoming conscious of your thoughts and the effects – both unkind and kind – they have on you and others is a Key Kind Leader Practice. There are three key behaviors associated with Thinking Kindly: *Always assume positive intent; Check your thoughts frequently and Consciously change unkind thoughts to kind ones.* You will learn about and practice each of the three in this chapter. As you'll see, the behaviors are interconnected and flow from each other as well.

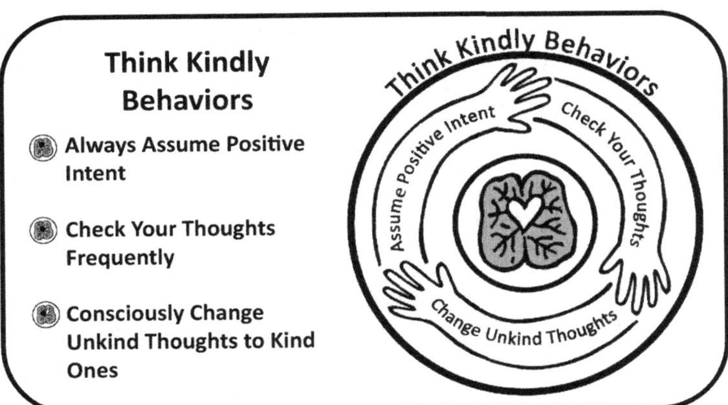

Figure 4.2 Think kindly behaviors.

Think Kindly Behavior 1: Always Assume Positive Intent

I was talking with my friend and not-for-profit leader Kathi Littman. After covering the formal Kind Leader interview questions, I asked Kathi if she had anything she'd like to add. After a moment of thought, Kathi said, "Our discussion brought something to mind. It may not fit in exactly, but would you mind if I told you the story anyways?"[1] Kathi then told me about a time when, early in her career, she worked for the Los Angeles Unified School District. She was driving a van with the school district's logo on it and had to stop to fill it up with gas. When Kathi came back from paying for the gas inside the station, she saw a person standing beside the van. From the looks of his clothing, he seemed to be homeless. Kathi felt worried: she was sure the person was going to ask her for money. So, with a sinking feeling in the pit of her stomach, she approached the van and the person. Only to find that her assumption was totally wrong. The homeless person didn't want to ask her for money, he wanted to give her money! Holding out a dollar bill he came up to Kathi and said, "Please take it for the kids, ma'am. It's for the kids". Having seen the logo on the van, the homeless man didn't want to ask for a donation … he wanted to make one!

Has something like this ever happened to you? That the first thing that's come into your mind is a negative thought or assumption? Like Kathi, it happens to everyone. And those negative, unkind thoughts and assumptions that arise about others' intentions influence the way you speak and act. Because Kind Leaders need to actively and deliberately model kind behavior, it's important that they don't make negative, unkind assumptions about their followers. That's why the first key Think Kindly behavior is *Always Assume Positive Intent.*

From the Think Kindly Key Leader Practice point of view, *Always Assume Positive Intent* means that the *first thoughts that come to a leader's mind in response to situations that occur are positive.* That means that even in a situation where a follower has made a mistake or acts in a way that isn't in accordance with a leader's expectations, instead of making a negative assumption about the person's intention, the leader assumes that the follower's intention was positive. That the follower planned to do their best and expected a good outcome, even if that didn't actually happen. (And in case you are thinking to yourself, "There are people who really don't have good intentions. What happens then?", you'll learn more about how Kind Leadership works in those circumstances in Chapter 8, When Things Don't Go Kindly on page 167.)

For leaders, it isn't easy to *always assume positive intent.* I know that from working with leaders and from leading myself. (I even worked for a manager who had a sign prominently displayed on her desk, beside a big bowl of candy, that said 'assume positive intent' to remind herself, and others, to do it!) This became even more evident to me when I asked people who I interviewed for this book to tell me a story about a time a leader acted kindly toward them. I was surprised to find that almost the same thing happened every time. People stopped, stared at me with a puzzled look on their face, and asked if I could give them a few minutes to think about it. I wondered to myself, "Why is it so hard for people to remember a specific time a leader was kind to them?" A couple of possibilities came to mind. Maybe, since leadership and kindness aren't often associated, the question wasn't something that people automatically connected with. Or, perhaps, they hadn't experienced leaders being kind to them (a very sad and worrisome thought), so didn't have any stories to tell. When I interviewed Pennie Saum, a continuous improvement leader working in a government agency, I asked her about what I was noticing. Pennie said, "It's not that I don't think there are instances of leaders being kind, I think we just remember negative, unkind things more easily".[2]

I agree with Pennie. Many people have what I call 'negative first impression'. I define this as an immediate, negative, unkind reaction to anything new and different that is presented to them. Put on your Follower

Hat and think back to a time that you were told about an impending change in your organization or in the way you were going to work. Did you immediately think of all the amazing possibilities that would come with that change? Or did you 'assume' the worst? If you are like most people, you will have assumed the worst. That's negative intent. To help you better recognize how often you first assume negative intent, go to this chapter's Practice Section and complete the exercise (Figure 4.3) on page 70. (You can stop and do the exercise now or continue reading and do it at the end of this chapter.)

There is actually scientific proof behind my belief that you'll first think the worst. It's called *negativity bias*, and because it's hardwired into your brain,[3] it means you may not even be conscious that your first assumptions about anything new are probably negative ones. In an article from *VeryWellMind*, negativity bias is defined as:

> The tendency not only to register negative stimuli more readily but also to dwell on these events. Also known as positive-negative asymmetry, this negativity bias means that we feel the sting of a rebuke more powerfully than we feel the joy of praise.[4]

The article goes on to list the effects of negativity bias and that due to it, people are more likely to:

- Remember traumatic experiences better than positive ones.
- Recall insults better than praise.
- React more strongly to negative stimuli.
- Think about negative things more frequently than positive ones.
- Respond more strongly to negative events than to equally positive ones.[5]

From the Kind Leader point of view, this is extremely significant. Take a close look at the above list and one of the first things you will notice is that all the thoughts and concerns generated aren't about others, they're about the person thinking them: How will I feel? How will I be affected? And even more significantly, how will I be *negatively* affected? What danger might I be in and what are the negative consequences for me? Biologically and neurologically, negativity bias focuses your thoughts on you. And about negative consequences or 'ends'.

KLC Stop & Think Point: As the old saying goes, 'the only thing constant is change'. Leaders are often the creators of change as well as the communicators of those changes. Put on your Leader Hat and think about whether, in times of change, you consider the effect on yourself or on others first.

As you've already learned, one of the Key Characteristics of Kind Leaders is that they *consider others first.* Thinking Kindly by *always assuming positive* intent is one of the behaviors that leaders can – and must – practice, so that instead of focusing first on themselves, they focus first on their followers and keeping their best interests at heart.

Think Kindly Behavior 2: Check Your Thoughts Frequently

The next Think Kindly Behavior, *Check Your Thoughts Frequently*, is a key behavior to practice to support *always assuming positive intent*. Because people are often not conscious of their thoughts, creating a way to 'check your thoughts' and make them conscious, helps you to see whether you are assuming positive intent or not, and the effects that your thoughts are having on you and on others.

As Pennie and I continued her Kind Leader Interview, Pennie told me a story about a time she was asked to work on a project with another department and noticed that she wasn't feeling very excited about the prospect. Since Pennie normally was excited about working on cross-departmental projects, she took a moment to *check her thoughts* and ask herself why she was feeling that way. After taking time to reflect, Pennie realized that this project seemed very similar to one she had worked on with that department in the past, and it hadn't gone as well as she would have liked. As Pennie continued to *check her thoughts*, she came to the conclusion that the reason she wasn't excited (a positive feeling) and, in fact, was worried (a negative feeling), was that it felt to her like when the other department was involved in a project, they always wanted to control everyone and how change was managed. "I wasn't assuming positive intent", Pennie said. "In fact, I realized that I was actually assuming the opposite, based on my previous experience".[6]

Taking time to *check your thoughts*, just as Pennie did, is the first step to making your unconscious assumptions, both negative and positive, conscious. And that's not just important because of negativity bias, but because of another kind of bias as well. And that's unconscious bias. In a SimplyPsychology.org article, unconscious bias, sometimes known as implicit bias, is defined as "attitudes and beliefs that occur outside of our conscious awareness and control".[7] The article describes a number of types of unconscious biases and also why people are prone to them.[8] Two of the main reasons are especially important to understanding why practicing *checking your thoughts frequently* is so important to *always assuming positive intent.* The first is that that the human brain looks for associations and patterns to make it easier to sort out the complex and complicated world. The second is that the human brain tends to take mental shortcuts to simplify the world and make quicker decisions.[9]

Looking back at Pennie's story, and her first reaction of being wary of working with the other department, it's easy to see both. Even though it was a new project (already susceptible to negativity bias), Pennie's brain made an association with previous projects she had worked on with that department. And her brain took a mental shortcut and assumed (negatively!) that working on the new project would be similar.

KLC Stop & Think Point: When have you been in a situation like Pennie's? Did you take a mental shortcut, or did you stop and reflect and check your thoughts? Put on your Leader Hat and think about what happened and what could have been different had you checked your thoughts to help you assume positive intent.

Because everyone is subject to unconscious bias, taking the time to stop and *check your thoughts frequently* is an essential Kind Leader behavior. "That's a great idea", you may be saying to yourself, "But my day is jam-packed busy. Work, family, social commitments. I hardly have time to breathe, let alone time to stop and check my thoughts". If this is you, don't worry. Noticing that you don't currently have time in your schedule to reflect (Kind Leader Characteristic 4) is the first step in creating a process that will allow you to take the time needed. A couple of tips and tricks that I've learned over the years are:

- *Create visual signals.* I wear a lot of bracelets and rings. Each of them has a symbolic meaning. Every time I see them, I'm reminded to stop and think. Just like the old-fashioned idea of tying a string around your finger. Think about what type of visual signal that you could use. A sticky note on your computer? A screen saver on your device? Try each one out and see what works for you.

- *Put dedicated time on your calendar. And stick to it!* I know that this sounds obvious, and too easy to be true, but it's not. Blocking time on your calendar, with a reminder, and then sticking to it, makes taking the time easier and helps makes stopping and checking your thoughts during those times habitual. Adding a special color will make the time stick out and act as a visual signal as well.
- *Make your practice visible to others.* As you learned in Chapter 2, the first of the Key Kind Leader Characteristics is to actively model kind behavior. Whether you're in a meeting, or having a discussion with a follower, asking for a break in the conversation so that you can stop and *check your thoughts* is a great way to both model the Think Kindly behavior and to create the time.

Checking your thoughts frequently supports *always assuming positive intent.* Because your brain is hardwired to think negatively first, look for associations and patterns and jump to mental conclusions, practicing this behavior is essential to thinking more kindly. You'll find an exercise to help you practice in this chapter's Practice Section (Figure 4.3) on page 70. (You can stop and do the exercise now or continue reading and do it at the end of this chapter.)

Checking your thoughts frequently also leads to the third Think Kindly Behavior, *consciously change unkind thoughts to kind ones.* As a person, and a leader, once you become aware of your unkind thoughts, you can make a conscious choice about what to do, including changing unkind thoughts to kind ones.

Think Kindly Behavior 3: Consciously Change Unkind Thoughts to Kind Ones

Like the two preceding Think Kindly Behaviors, being able to *Consciously Change Unkind Thoughts to Kind Ones* takes practice. And lots of it. Because humans are hardwired to focus on the negative first and to look for patterns and take mental leaps based on those assumptions, unkind thinking can become habitual. The good thing though is that people aren't prisoners of those unkind thoughts. They can consciously change them to kind ones.

As Pennie and I continued our discussion about the cross-departmental project, I asked what effect stopping and checking her thoughts had. Pennie said, "As soon as I realized that my negative reaction was caused by my thoughts that the other department would try to control us, I consciously chose to think differently instead. I thought about all the possible reasons I might not know about that the other department might feel like they needed to be in control: Like maybe the outcomes were on their performance goals and they were afraid of what might happen if they didn't make them; or they were trying to make sure that others didn't get in trouble if the project wasn't successful. And I also thought about how they might feel about working with us on the project. Maybe it hadn't been a great experience for them in the past either. And consciously changing my thinking didn't just affect what I thought. It also affected what I did! Instead of just sitting around and worrying about things, I reached out to the other department's leader to set up a meeting to talk directly. That way I could build a bridge with kindness".[10] Once Pennie could 'see' her unkind thoughts clearly, she was able to practice the third Kind Leader behavior and choose to consciously change those unkind thoughts into kind ones.

As a leader, conscious practice won't just help you think more kindly on a one-off basis, it will help each time an unkind thought comes to mind, as it did in Pennie's situation. Practicing *consciously changing unkind thoughts into kind ones* can also make thinking kindly more habitual. This happens through something called neuroplasticity, the brain's ability to change and adapt in response to new experiences. In an article on Positive Psychology.com, the ability of our brain to develop new neural pathways throughout life is explained: "When we learn something new, we create new connections between our neurons. We rewire our brains to adapt to new circumstances. This happens on a daily basis, but it's also something that we can encourage and stimulate".[11] What's one of the best ways to 'encourage and stimulate' those new neural pathways? By practicing the desired new behavior over and over again.[12]

When I asked business owner Karidja Sakanogo to tell me about a time that she acted kindly as a leader, she told me about her experience being a flight attendant. "As a flight attendant, I had to make the conscious choice to put my personal feelings aside, and to think kindly about people all the time. That's what allowed me to give each of them great service".[13] For Kind Leaders, practicing *consciously changing unkind thoughts to kind ones* is extremely important because it helps to create the habit of thinking kindly in the first place. When leaders are consciously thinking kindly, they are more likely to assume positive intent! And, as we will see in the next two chapters, thinking kindly leads both to speaking and acting in kinder ways as well.

KLC Stop & Think Point: Consciously changing unkind thoughts to kind ones means a leader needs to be deliberate in their practice. Put on your Leader Hat and think about how you will create a time, place and system to note your negative, unkind thoughts and the positive, kind ones to replace them with.

To improve your ability to *consciously change unkind thoughts into kind ones*, you'll need to be deliberate. Because unkind thoughts come first, it may take you a few tries to think of a kind one to replace it with. It also might seem that finding a kind thought is impossible. When that happens, here's a couple of suggestions of what to do:

- *Walk a mile in the other person's shoes*. Like Pennie did, imagine you are the person you are having the unkind thoughts about. Think about all the possible positive reasons they might be acting as they are.
- *Ask others for help*. If you get stuck thinking about a kind thought to replace an unkind one with, ask a colleague or friend for help. Describe the situation, explain that you are having difficulty thinking kindly and see what they have to say.

You will also need to create a system to note down unkind thoughts and then the kind thoughts you consciously replace them with. You can use the notes function of a device or a paper notebook. Just make sure it's something that you have with you and ready at all times. You'll find an exercise to help you with this in this chapter's Practice Section (Figure 4.5) on page 74. (You can stop and do the exercise now or continue reading and do it at the end of this chapter.)

Kind Leaders Have Best Interests at Heart!

Throughout this chapter, you've seen that practicing the three Key Think Kindly Behaviors will help you become more conscious of when you are thinking kindly and when you aren't. But practicing these key behaviors aren't just important to help you personally become a kinder leader. They're an important part of creating a culture of trust.

Thinking Kindly Focuses Leaders on Others

For leaders, thinking kindly about others is extremely important because as we've learned, in order to create a culture of trust, leaders need to have their followers' best interests at heart. When leaders assume negative intent, don't check their thoughts for unconscious bias and don't work to change unkind thoughts to kind ones, it's likely that they will remain focused on potential negative consequences and end results in different situations for *them*. Had Pennie not taken the time to check her thoughts and change unkind thoughts to kind ones, she might have remained suspicious, fearful and worried about the other departmental leader's motives. As you saw in Chapter 3, though, fear and kindness don't go together. When leaders practice the Think Kindly Behaviors, they're both modeling kind behavior for their followers and considering others first, laying the groundwork for a culture of trust.

Kind Leaders Think Kindly about Themselves as Well

Thinking more kindly takes a great deal of practice over time. No one, and no leader, thinks kindly at all times. Practicing the Think Kindly behaviors will help you think more kindly of others and can – and should – also be applied to yourself! As you practice, when you notice that despite your best intentions, you've slipped back into old habits and assumed negative intent, stop and reflect deeply about it (Kind Leader Characteristic 4). Focus on the means and work on understanding what happened in the situation so you can be more conscious of it next time. Then be as kind to yourself as a Kind Leader would be to others in this situation. Another opportunity to practice the Think Kindly Behaviors is right around the corner! I can personally guarantee it!

Practice: Practical Exercises to Use to Turn Your Thoughts into Action

Automatically Thinking Kindly isn't easy. For leaders, or for anyone! Because your thoughts aren't readily visible and negative thinking patterns are hardwired into your brain, dedicating time and attention to practicing the three Think Kindly Behaviors is the best way to help you to get started on making thinking kindly a habit. Because practicing these behaviors is so important, I've added extra exercises for you to do in this section. You can complete them here, or use your device or a notebook.

Exercise 1: Always Assume Positive Intent: Recognizing Negative First Impression

Recognizing negative first impression takes practice. With your Follower Hat on, think about situations at work, at home and in the community when

Practice recognizing negative first impression Put on your Follower Hat and think back to a time a change was announced in your organization. What were the first thoughts that came to mind? Were they negative or positive?		
Impending change	**What specific thoughts came into your mind?**	**Negative or positive first?**
Work:	Thoughts:	
Home:	Thoughts:	
Community:	Thoughts:	

Figure 4.3 Negative thoughts usually come before positive ones.

you were told a change was about to happen. What were the first thoughts that came into your mind? Were they positive, or were they negative?

Bonus Exercise

Focusing on yourself, and how you may be negatively affected in a situation can cause a leader to get stuck in assuming negative intent. Write a list of things that you are afraid of and the negative consequences that might occur. Example: *I'm afraid that if I miss my revenue target, I won't get my bonus. If that happens, I'm not sure how I'll pay for my daughter's college tuition*. Making your fears visible will help you become more conscious of things and situations that can trigger you to assume negative intent. Write your list here:

Exercise 2: Check Your Thoughts Frequently: Making Unkind Thoughts Conscious

Each day, you have many opportunities to stop and check your thoughts to make unkind ones conscious. A great way to practice is by noticing how you feel about each email you receive before you open and read it! Depending on the situation, switch between your Leader and Follower Hats. Write down your unkind thoughts and assumptions and the reasons you feel that way. Are you afraid? Thinking of ends, not means? Other reasons?

Practice checking your thoughts frequently Go to your email in-bin. Before opening each new email, look at the subject line and the sender. Notice how you feel. Write down any unkind thoughts and assumptions you have. Stop and reflect on why you feel and think that way. Write the reasons down. Practice this every day for a week. Do the same for phone calls and people you interact with.		
Feelings	**Unkind thoughts and assumptions**	**Reasons**

Figure 4.4 Practice checking your thoughts frequently to make the unconscious conscious.

Bonus Exercise

Although thoughts aren't always easily visible, certain types of thoughts trigger certain physical symptoms and actions which are visible. When my son was young, before he lost his temper, he would clench and unclench his fists. I helped him learn to recognize that when he started doing that, it was time to take a break and do something calming! You can do the same thing. Monitor your physical reactions closely. Note what is happening when you are thinking unkindly. Are you pacing? Does your stomach hurt? Do you get a pain in your neck or shoulder? Recognizing these physical symptoms can help you notice when you need to stop and check your thoughts. Pay close attention and write your list of signals here:

Exercise 3: Change Unkind Thoughts to Kind Ones

Changing your initial unkind thoughts to kind ones can be challenging. Using the unkind thoughts from Exercise 2, write down at least one kind thought to replace it with. If you have trouble thinking of a kind thought, ask someone else to give you a suggestion.

Practice consciously changing unkind thoughts to kind ones Using the list of unkind thoughts and assumptions from Exercise 2, practice changing unkind thoughts to kind ones. Write each unkind thought down, and then write at least one kind thought to replace it with. Practice every day for at least a week.	
Unkind thought	**Kind thought to replace it**

Figure 4.5 Practice consciously changing unkind thoughts to kind ones.

Bonus Exercise

Think back to situations in your life when people didn't act as you hoped they would. Write the situations down and the unkind thoughts you felt about them. Put yourself in the other person's shoes and think about the situation from their perspective. Challenge yourself to think about at least three different kind ways you could have thought about the situation instead. Write your list here:

Reflection: What Would You Do? Kind Leader Practice Scenarios

Now that you've had the opportunity to read the ideas and theory presented in the Discussion section and do the Practice exercises, it's time to reflect on what you've learned and proactively plan how to apply those learnings.

I'm sure you are wondering how Kay'La Janson and Kevin Landrell are doing in their quest to lead kindly. Let's check in and see.

Practicing Thinking Kindly Takes Practice

Scenario 1: Kay'La's Story: If at First You Don't Think Kindly ...

It had been a busy six months for Kay'La Janson and the team at Codstom Industries. Looking out the window of her office, Kay'La thought to herself, "I can't believe how quickly time flies. Must mean I'm having fun! But it's been so busy, I guess I haven't had time to notice!" Between helping her executive team get sorted out, working to mend broken relationships with suppliers and customers, Kay'La had hardly had a minute to herself. "Things are definitely getting better though", Kay'la thought as she continued to reflect. "The team is bringing up things that they would have been afraid to in past, we're getting fewer customer complaints and employee turnover is slowing. Things really do seem to be stabilizing. I knew that it would be a lot of effort, but I guess, until you do something, you don't really know exactly how much".

Kay'La turned away from the window, sat down at her desk and glanced at her calendar. Looked like every minute of her day was booked. "Going to be a sprint today", she said quietly to herself. "Maybe that's why I'm feeling a little 'grumpy around the edges'…" 'Grumpy around the edges' was a term that Kay'La used when she was feeling out of sorts but couldn't quite put her finger on why. Normally, when she felt like that, she'd take some time to reflect, but today didn't look like it was going to be that day. Just as she was picking up the phone to make her ten o'clock call, Eric Rogers, the Vice President of Human Resources burst into her office, with Anderson following close behind. "Eric" Anderson said, "Kay'La has a phone call scheduled with Renton Inc., and she doesn't have time to see you right now". But before anyone could stop him, Eric blurted out angrily, "Kay'La, I told you that I was dealing with the union situation. I had it under control. Why would you go tell them that we'd be happy to sit down and talk some more? I had it all wrapped up and ready to go. I don't need your help, and I certainly didn't need you getting involved at this late stage of the game".

Kay'La could feel her temper rising. She put down the phone, looked up at Eric and…

Now It's Your Turn to Reflect and Apply

Put on your Leader Hat and think about what you would do in this situation. How could you stop yourself from thinking unkindly and jumping to conclusions? How could you change unkind thoughts to kind ones? How could you respond to Eric in a way that would model kind behavior? Write your ideas here:

Scenario 2: Kevin's Story: 'Think, Think Again ...'

Kevin was feeling pretty proud of himself. Six months had passed by and he'd made it! There had been a lot of challenges, and a lot of learning, but he hadn't crumbled! The team's surveys were up, customers were even starting to give the team a compliment here and there, Jaden had settled in and even Molly's attitude had made a marked improvement. Looking out from his cubicle, Kevin could see Jaden and Molly looking at Jaden's computer screen together.

"I can't believe it! I guess hard work really does pay off", Kevin thought to himself. "I'm so happy with all the progress the team has made in the past six months. Jaden is making great progress learning and customers love him, and Molly has really turned herself around. Here's to the next six months! It was tough to get here, but I'm sure it will get easier every day from now on!" Just then Kevin's moment of happy reflection was interrupted by Molly's angry voice. "Jaden, if I told you once, I told you a million times. You can't use that field with international orders ... only on domestic ones. Why don't you ever pay attention?"

"Oh no", thought Kevin. "Just when things were going so well. Why does this have to happen? Are we back where we started?"

Kevin stood up, walked out of his cubicle and ...

Now It's Your Turn to Reflect and Apply

Put on your Leader Hat. What would you do in this situation knowing Jaden and Molly's past history? What could you do to change any unkind thoughts you have into kind ones? How would you approach Jaden and Molly? Write about what you would do here:

Chapter 4 Kind-Points

- *The Three Key Kind Leader Practices are Think Kindly, Speak Kindly and Act Kindly.* Each Key Practice has three associated behaviors. The Practices are the 'how' of kind leadership, so it's important to practice them, not just read about them and have a theoretical understanding. Real learning comes from turning theory into practice.
- *Think Kindly Key Behaviors.* The three Think Kindly Key Behaviors are: *Always assume positive intent; Check your thoughts frequently and Consciously change unkind thoughts to kind ones.* They are interconnected, influence and flow from each other.
- *Always Assume Positive Intent* means that the *first thoughts that come to a leader's mind in response to situations that occur are positive.* Assuming positive intent isn't easy because of negativity bias, the biological preponderance to focus on the negative in order to stay safe.
- *Check Your Thoughts Frequently* helps leaders make unconscious thoughts and biases conscious, so they can see whether they are assuming positive intent or not. Creating visual signals and dedicated time to reflect are key to practicing this behavior.
- *Consciously Change Unkind Thoughts to Kind Ones* takes a lot of practice because humans are hardwired to focus on the negative, look for patterns and take mental leaps based on those assumptions. However, through consistent and constant practice, leaders can create a new kind thinking habit through neuroplasticity.
- *Thinking Kindly Supports a Culture of Trust.* When leaders think kindly of others, they are less likely to focus on potential negative consequences for themselves. Focusing on others and their best interests both helps to reduce fear and create a culture of trust.

Notes

1 Personal interview with Kathi Littman on December 14, 2020.
2 Personal interview with Pennie Saum on December 23, 2020.
3 Activation of the right inferior frontal/insular cortex and the amygdala have been shown to be more active when to stimuli rated as negative versus positive. A. Vaish, T. Grossmann and A. Woodward. Not All Emotions Are Created Equal: The Negativity Bias in Social-Emotional Development. *Psychological Bulletin*134(3) (2008):383–403. doi:10.1037/0033-2909.134.3.383 p. 3 Downloaded on December 20, 2020.
4 www.verywellmind.com/negative-bias-4589618 Downloaded on October 16, 2020.
5 Ibid.
6 Personal interview with Pennie Saum on December 23, 2020.
7 C. Ruhl, (July 1, 2020). Implicit or Unconscious Bias. *Simply Psychology*. www.simplypsychology.org/implicit-bias.html Downloaded on December 21, 2020.
8 Ibid.
9 Ibid.
10 Personal interview with Pennie Saum on December 23, 2020.
11 https://positivepsychology.com/neuroplasticity/ Downloaded on December 23, 2020.
12 www.edutopia.org/neuroscience-brain-based-learning-neuroplasticity Downloaded December 22, 2020.
13 Personal interview with Karidja Sakanogo on December 5, 2020.

Chapter 5

Speak Kindly

Use Words of Encouragement and Growth

If speaking kindly to plants makes them grow, imagine what speaking kindly to people can do!

Unknown

Discussion – Words Matter: Choose and Use Yours Kindly

I'd like you to take a moment, put on your Follower Hat and think back to a time a leader has spoken kindly to you. Maybe they complimented your work or praised your effort or thanked you for your commitment to the organization and its customers. How did you feel? I'm going to imagine happy and proud! I bet that you walked out of the meeting with a spring in your step, your head held high and a song in your heart. Your good mood probably lasted throughout the rest of the day and probably even rubbed off on others at work and at home.

Now I'd like you to think about the opposite situation. A time when a leader spoke unkindly to you. Perhaps they were dismissive, belittled your efforts or even used a derogatory term or raised their voice. How did you feel then? I'm going to guess that you were upset and angry. After the meeting, at work and at home, perhaps you took out your anger and

DOI: 10.4324/9781003141433-5

frustration on others. Maybe you even used the exact same unkind words your leader did…

Although leaders aren't always conscious of it, the words they use carry a lot of weight. Those words also travel fast, and they travel far, within the organization and beyond. Jamie Flinchbaugh, a continuous improvement leader, commented about this on a social media post I wrote. Jamie said,

> I find that many leaders actually under-appreciate their influence. They think their power is in decision making, but their words and even questions have tremendous influence, more so than they think (otherwise they would treat them with more care and thoughtfulness).[1]

Because the words that leaders use have such a strong effect, both on individual followers and on creating an organization's culture, learning how to consciously and deliberately speak kindly is essential for Kind Leaders.

Speaking Kindly Is the Second of The Three Key Kind Leader Practices

In this chapter, you'll learn about and practice the three key behaviors of the second of the Key Kind Leader Practices: *Speak Kindly.* The Speak Kindly behaviors are: *Choose your words kindly; Use a kind tone of voice and If it's not kind, don't say it.* As you'll see throughout this chapter, practicing the three key Speak Kindly behaviors will help you become

Figure 5.1 Speak Kindly Behaviors.

more deliberate about the specific words you choose and *how* you use them, including tone of voice and body language. Like the Think Kindly behaviors, The Speak Kindly behaviors are interconnected, flow from and influence each other.

Speak Kindly Behavior 1: Choose Your Words Kindly

Leaders spend a lot of time speaking. Whether talking directly to followers to give them directions or weighing in with an opinion, leading a group discussion in a meeting, giving a company-wide speech or sending email, studies suggest that every day, leaders spend about 80 percent of their time in some sort of form of communication.[2] With that statistic in mind, take a moment, put your Leader Hat on and ask yourself this question: How often, as a leader, are you totally conscious of the words that you are using? Be totally honest. Don't be surprised if it's not a large percentage. Most people don't choose the words they use deliberately in every situation. Words stem from thoughts, and because, as you saw in Chapter 4, a lot of thinking is unconscious, word choice is often unconscious too. That's why *Choose your words kindly* is the first key Speak Kindly behavior.

Leaders' Words Travel Far, Fast and Carry a Lot of Weight

Not only do leaders spend a large percentage of their time speaking, but the words they use travel fast, travel far and carry a lot of weight. Most organizations have some version of 'the grapevine': something a leader says in a meeting at home office in one city travels quickly, office to office, through these unofficial, person-to-person networks. Additionally, leaders' words are often amplified through internal and external social media channels. Whether posted as an update on a company's intranet, or tweeted and retweeted, followers have the opportunity to hear and see a leader's words over and over again. As a leader, you need to remember that nothing you say is really ever 'off the record' and that you never really know who might be listening to your words. If you aren't conscious of the words you choose to use, and don't speak kindly, your unkind words can both negatively affect individual followers and create a culture of fear.

When I started working with holistic dental practice leader Michelle Jorgensen (who you met in Chapter 1), Michelle told me about an ongoing problem in her office. The problem was twofold. First, as Michelle went about her day, team members often stopped her in the hallway between patients or asked for a few moments of her time in private, to complain about their coworkers: speaking unkindly about what others were doing, how they were acting and what they were saying. The second part of the problem had to do with a situation surrounding the office's weekly management meeting, a portion of which was devoted to talking about which team members were doing what incorrectly. When she left each of the Tuesday meetings, as she walked through the office, Michelle noticed that team members seemed tense and unhappy. When she asked one of them about it, the person told Michelle that while managers were meeting, all of the other team members were worried about what management was saying about them. Because they knew that part of each meeting was devoted to talking about what team members were doing wrong, every Tuesday, they worried that management was talking about *them*. When Michelle told me about this, she said, "The whole situation just isn't good. The feeling in the office is one of palpable mistrust. It doesn't go with our Total Care Values and the culture I want for my practice".[3]

As Michelle and I talked through the situation, I pointed out something that I had noticed in our coaching sessions: that Michelle often told me stories about the team members who worked for her, what people had done wrong and how frustrated she was with them. And the words she, herself, used often weren't very kind. After a moment of deep silence, Michelle said to me:

> Oh my goodness. You are entirely right. No wonder my team members are coming to complain to me about others. No wonder people aren't speaking kindly. Including my management team. I'm the leader, and that's the model I'm giving them. If I want them to change the way they're speaking and the words they're using, I'm going to have to change what I'm saying, and how I'm saying it.[4]

Michelle's words and how she used them provided a model for how everyone in the practice talked to each other. That's because how people speak to each other is part of an organizations culture, *how things are expected and allowed to be done around here*. Because Michelle wasn't conscious of the words she was using, instead of deliberately choosing kind word ones that would create the culture of trust that she wanted, her words had the opposite effect.

KLC Stop & Think Point: Leaders spend a lot of time talking. And their words carry a lot of weight. Put on your Leader Hat and think about a recent conversation you had with a follower. Did your words (and the way that you used them) provide a model for the way you'd like others in your organization to speak?

As a leader, being able to choose your words kindly means that first you need to be conscious of the words that you are using now. Once you become conscious of those words, you can analyze them and see whether they are kind or not, and whether they are the words that you want your team to use. Because you can be sure, whatever words you use, your team will use too. To help you become conscious of the words that you are using now, and whether they are perceived by others as kind or not, go to this chapter's Practice Section and complete the exercise (Figure 5.3) on page 94. (You can stop and do the exercise now or continue reading and do it at the end of this chapter.)

What Kind of Words Are Kind?

Choosing your words kindly doesn't just mean avoiding those that are obviously unkind, like swear words or racial slurs. It means being conscious of how each of the words you use is understood and perceived by *others* (Kind Leader Characteristic 3). As a leader, in order to do this, you'll need to consider both the *denotative* and *connotative* meanings of your words. If you're not familiar with these concepts, the *denotative* meaning of a word is its exact translation in the dictionary: its literal meaning. As well as having a denotative meaning, many words also have emotional undertones, feelings and other associations tied to them. Those are the word's *connotative* meanings. Connotative meanings fall into three categories: neutral, positive and negative. Neutral connotative meanings are close to the standard, denotative meaning. Having a positive connotation means that a word has positive feelings or emotions associated with it, and having a negative connotation means that a word is associated with negative feelings or emotions.[5]

Here's an example. A little while ago, as part of a Women In Lean – Our Table Learning Interchange,[6] business owner Michelle Hlywa presented some work she was doing creating an assessment tool. As part of the tool,

Michelle used birds to symbolically describe different personality traits. As I listened to Michelle talk about the Dove, I was struck by the fact that words she was using like 'armed', 'targeted' and others with military references, didn't seem to fit with the 'love' symbolism of the dove. There seemed to be a disconnect between denotative and connotative meanings. When I asked Michelle about it, she said, "Before I started my own business, I worked for an organization that hired a lot of people from the defense industry. Those were the words we regularly used. Let me think about how they go with this work".[7] As a leader, it's just as important to consider the connotative meanings of the words you are using as the denotative ones. Otherwise, while you think you are saying one thing, followers might interpret another.

Because leaders' words travel fast, far and carry a lot of weight, making sure to choose words with kind meanings is something leaders need to deliberately spend time on. Kind words are those that have neutral or positive connotative meanings and that make followers feel positive and encouraged. And because a leaders' words create culture as well, they need to be words that don't have a negative, fearful connotation and they need to focus on the means, not the ends.

Here are some ideas about how to go about deliberately choosing your words kindly:

- *Choose human words.* As you've seen throughout this book, people are never numbers and shouldn't be referred to as such. Instead of referring to clients by a number (like they did at the organization in which the leader's favorite saying was 'the number is the number') use your clients' actual names. "Mr. Jones from The Southwest Store called", is kinder than "Client #B238 left a message".
- *Choose 'living' words.* People aren't resources. Resources are non-living things that can be depleted and used up. Human beings, when treated kindly, learn, grow and appreciate over time. Instead of using terms like Full Time Equivalents (FTEs), heads or human capital, simply refer to people as people.
- *Choose organic words.* Organizations aren't machines. Whether business, social or political, they're made up of living human beings. Don't describe them with mechanical words. Instead of using terms like 'function like a well-oiled machine', 'drive results', 'move the needle' and 'laser-focused', choose words like 'nurture', 'blossom' and 'grow'. Words from the living, organic world.

- *Choose words that elicit trust and that don't incite fear.* Words and phrases with unkind connotations like 'targeted', 'brutal', 'aggressive', 'cut-throat' and 'front-line' (a military reference) can create a culture of fear. So can the word 'power'. Choose, instead words and phrases like 'caring', 'open-door', 'helpful' and 'customer-serving' that have positive connotations that cultivate trust.
- *Choose words that focus on the means, not the ends.* Instead of using words and terms that focus people on the ends such as 'results-based' and 'bottom-line focused', choose terms such as 'process-oriented', and 'effort'. And instead of holding people 'accountable' (a numbers word) to the ends, how about 'helping' them with the means instead?

As you become more conscious about the words you are choosing, you will probably realize that you don't know how some (or many) of them are being construed by your followers. When that happens, here are a couple of things you can do. The first is to ask your followers directly how they feel about words that are commonly used in your organization. That's because although the denotative meaning of the word you are using might describe what you want it to, the connotative meaning followers ascribe to it might not be. The second is to *stop and check your thoughts frequently.* If you aren't sure a word and its associations are kind, spend time deliberately reflecting on it. Look up the denotative and connotative meanings to make sure they are in line with the kind culture of trust you want to create. Then ask your followers what they think.

KLC Stop & Think Point: Do you know how the words you use are interpreted by your followers? Put on your Leader Hat and think about words and phrases commonly used in your organization from your followers' point of view. Do you think they have positive or negative connotations? How can you find out?

For leaders, consciously and deliberately choosing and using kind words needs to be an ongoing practice. Helping others in your organization become more conscious of the words that they are using, and then deliberately choose to use kind ones, is also an important part of a leader's Speak Kindly practice. Once Michelle Jorgensen came to the realization that she was using unkind words to complain about team members and their performance, she called a staff meeting, explained the situation and set new ground rules: Starting a sentence with a team members' name, followed by a negative comment, wasn't allowed anymore. What it was to be replaced with was a description of the situation and how it was impacting customers or the business. Michelle followed these new ground rules herself, and soon others in the office did as well. Instead of focusing on the ends, blaming people and creating a culture in which team members were afraid, Michelle provided and modeled new words and a kinder way of speaking that focused on the means and promoted a culture of trust.[8]

It's up to you, as a leader, to define what words can be used in the organization, which words cannot be, and what words should replace those with unkind connotations that aren't to be used. To help you begin to do this, go to this chapter's Practice Section and complete the exercise (Figure 5.3) on page 95. (You can stop and do the exercise now or continue reading and do it at the end of this chapter.)

Speak Kindly Behavior 2: Use a Kind Tone of Voice

As I'm sure you've experienced, leaders don't just create and convey meaning through words alone. Much of what followers understand about what a leader is saying is conveyed by *how* they say it. Their tone of voice, body language and writing style all carry meanings that are interpreted by followers. That's why *Use a Kind Tone of Voice* is the second of the Key Speak Kindly Behaviors.

Exactly how much meaning is carried through body language, tone of voice and actual words? Studies have shown that the percentages are about 55 for body language, 38 for tone of voice and only 7 percent for the actual words spoken.[9] Think about it. As a leader, that means about 93 percent of what you are saying to your followers doesn't come from your word choice, it comes from how followers perceive how you say what you say. Research also shows that when there is an apparent difference between the meaning of words being spoken and the nonverbal communication of the speaker, people will weigh what's being communicated non-verbally, more heavily.[10] That's because, as Carol Kinsey Gorman states in an article on Forbes.com, nonverbal communication "Will reveal underlying emotions, motives, and feelings. In fact, people will evaluate most of the emotional content of your message, not by what you say but by your nonverbal signals".[11] Kinsey Gorman goes on to say that in one half-hour business discussion, "Two people can send over eight hundred different nonverbal signals".[12] For leaders, being conscious of their body language, tone of voice, and the effects those have on others, is just as important as paying attention to the words they are choosing to use.

Like word choice, many people aren't conscious of their body language or tone of voice. A few years ago, I was working with Doug Wotherspoon, a member of a college's senior executive team. As we visited team members who served customers directly, I started to notice something. Doug is very tall! Most of the team members he was speaking with were seated at desks. As Doug stood beside their desks, he actually appeared, through no fault of his own, to be towering over them. As Doug continued to enthusiastically ask questions, I could see that many of the team members looked uncomfortable. Then I realized that although Doug's questions weren't being asked in any type of accusatory way, because there was such a great difference in hierarchical power, and because Doug was so tall, it was making team members feel as if they were being interrogated. I pointed this out to Doug and asked what he could do to change his body language. At the next session, instead of standing, Doug knelt down on the floor beside each person's desk. Instead of towering over people, Doug was now face to face with them, on their level. As well as changing the physical dynamic, that small change in body language changed the power dynamic and the nature of the entire dialogue. It no longer felt like an inquisition, but a discussion among equals instead. Years later, Doug and I talked about this. He said:

> My knees and pants have had a lot of wear and tear since then! But it's been a practice that I've continued because, as a leader, kneeling beside someone changes the whole mood of the interaction. Often the person asks if I would like a chair. When they help to find a chair, they are inviting me into their world and the conversations tend to last much longer and be far more encompassing, all I think because of the invitation to join them.[13]

Tone of voice is like that too. How people interpret the meaning of the actual words being said changes depending on the tone of the voice of the person saying them. Put on your Follower Hat and think about a time when your leader said something to you like, "Great job. It's not exactly what I was looking for but I really appreciate your effort". How did you feel? If you felt good, it was probably because your leader used a calm, friendly, positive tone of voice. Or maybe you didn't feel so good. Perhaps it was because your leader used a harsh, sarcastic or accusatory tone voice when speaking. Even though your leaders' words may have been kind and focused on the 'means', what you probably read from their unkind tone of voice was that what they were really focused was on the 'ends'.

Like body language, how your tone of voice is perceived by others isn't something that you may be as conscious of as you should be. And tone of voice doesn't refer to just one thing. It has a number of different elements including breath, volume and speed. The way you breath when talking can influence how others perceive your psychological frame of mind. If you are breathing quickly you might be anxious. Slow and steady, calm. Huffing and puffing can signal anger and upset. The volume you speak to someone with can convey how you feel about your relationship with them. A loud tone of voice or shouting will be perceived as anger by the other person. A quiet tone can convey concern or fear. The speed at which you speak can suggest your emotional state. Speaking quickly can be perceived as a lack of interest in others. Speaking slowly can be felt as condescending: you are speaking slowly because you don't believe others will understand.[14] Pitch, both high and low, also affects how others read your tone of voice. A low, deep pitch can be perceived as commanding and authoritarian. A drop in pitch at the end of a sentence is also associated with a command. Higher pitches convey friendlier communication and a rise in pitch at the end of a sentence usually signals a question or inquiry.[15] As you can see, as a leader, if you aren't conscious of, and deliberately choosing your body language and tone of voice, no matter what words you choose, followers aren't going to 'get the message' of kindness.

KLC Stop & Think Point: How often do you pay attention to your body language and tone of voice? Put on your Leader Hat and reflect on how followers react to you when you speak with them. How much of their reaction comes from your words? How much from your body language and tone of voice?

Here are some ways for you to become more conscious of and choose kinder body language and tone of voice:

- *Watch yourself on video.* Have someone tape you in a variety of situations. Speaking one on one with followers, in group staff meetings, and while giving a speech. Then put on your Follower Hat and watch the video with the sound on. Listen to your tone of voice (breath, volume, speed and pitch). What do hear? How does it make you feel? Next, turn off the sound and watch the video again. Put your Leader Hat on and watch how your followers in the video respond. What does it tell you about what your body language and tone are conveying?
- *Ask your friends and family for help.* Ask friends and family members to point out body language and tone of voice habits that they notice. For instance, do you tap your foot when you are impatient? Do you do things that could be perceived as dismissive such as roll your eyes or look up over your glasses when someone says something you don't agree with? Point an angry finger? Do you frequently check your devices while others are speaking? Do you interrupt instead of letting other finish what they are saying? How about your tone of voice? Is it abrupt? Accusatory? Sarcastic? Overly loud or aggressive? Listen carefully to what they have to say and then …
- *Practice in front of the mirror.* Once you become conscious of the body language and tone of voice habits that are preventing your words from being perceived kindly, deliberately replace them with body language and tone that convey kindness. Practice in front of the mirror so that you can 'see' and hear what you look like. Put on your Follower Hat while practicing and reflect on how the changes you are making make you feel. Then try out your changes in reality, and 'see' what happens.
- *Be mindful of emotional situations.* Because body language and tone of voice convey emotions and feelings, it can be harder to moderate yours when in stressful and emotional situations. Know what your triggers are (things and situations that make you angry and upset) and take special care in situations where you know those things will be happening. The best advice I ever got about communicating in stressful situations was to lean back in my chair and consciously relax my muscles. I got the advice a long time ago, and still practice it to this day.

- *Check your email.* Leaders spend a lot of time 'speaking' in written form. Check your emails for unkind tone (and unkind words as well). Are you using all capitals? Followers may feel like you are shouting at them. Short, curt sentences? Followers may feel like they have come up 'short' and you are irritated with them. Do your sentences sound sarcastic? If you aren't sure if your email tone of voice sounds kind, ask someone else to read it before you send it.

As you can see in Figure 5.2, Speaking Kindly is the combination of kind words, kind body language and kind tone of voice. It requires you, as a leader to be conscious of, and deliberate in, your use of all three. As a leader, you also need to define the types of body language and tone of voice that are acceptable for others to use. Actively modeling those yourself will go a long way. You will also have to point out kindly when others aren't using body language and tone kindly. To help you define kind body language and tone of voice in different situations, go to this chapter's Practice Section and complete the exercises (Figures 5.4 and 5.5) on pages 95 and 97. (You can stop and do them now or continue reading and do it at the end of this chapter.)

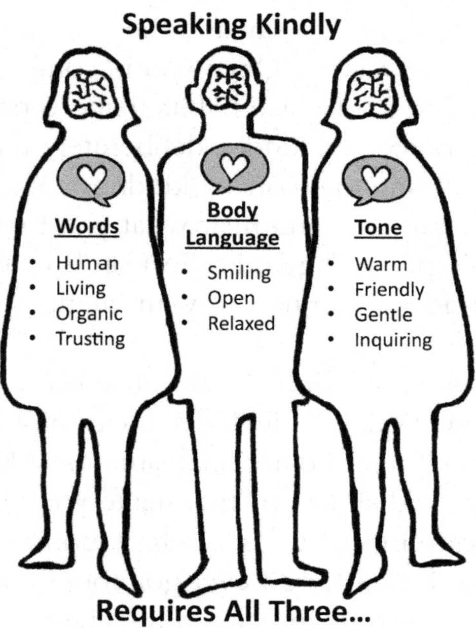

Figure 5.2 Speaking Kindly = Kind Words + Kind Body Language + Kind Tone.

Speak Kindly Behavior 3: If It's Not Kind, Don't Say It!

For Kind Leaders, speaking kindly doesn't just mean choosing your words kindly and using a kind tone of voice. Knowing when to speak, and when not to, is just as important. Because leaders speak so often and are often expected to speak first, this can take quite a lot of practice. That's why the third Speak Kindly key behavior is *If it's not kind, don't say it!*

Kathi Littman, who you met in Chapter 4, told me a great story about this during her Kind Leader interview. During the COVID-19 crisis, she had called her leadership team together virtually to discuss an important issue. Although she thought she had explained the issue, and her expectations clearly, as she listened to her team members debate back and forth, she didn't feel like they were where she thought they should be. As she continued to listen in on their discussion, Kathi could feel herself getting frustrated and upset. First, she thought about breaking in with her point of view, but as she *stopped and checked her thoughts*, she realized that if she did, her word choice might not be kind, and that her tone of voice might not be either. So, instead of speaking up in the moment, Kathi decided to graciously leave the conversation. She knew that she could always talk to each person individually later, and that she needed time to reflect in order to think about what to say to each one, and how to say it.[16] Because leaders' words travel fast, far and carry a lot of weight, it's important for them to know when staying silent is the kindest thing to do.

KLC Stop & Think Point: Put on your Leader Hat and think back to a time when results weren't as you expected and you spoke unkindly. What would have happened If you'd focused on the means instead, and refrained from speaking in the moment? What would have been different for your team, and for you?

Practicing modeling the behavior of refraining from speaking unkindly is just as important as choosing and using words, body language and tone of voice kindly. I'm sure you are familiar with the phrase, 'sticks and stones may break my bones, but words will never hurt me'. Unfortunately, that's not the case. Being spoken to unkindly, especially by a leader, is extremely hurtful. And causes a lot of fear. Unfortunately, I'm sure that if you put on your Follower Hat, you will be able to think back to times when you were afraid that your leader was going to say something unkind to you. Those words sting, and they tend to stick as well. Pennie Saum and I talked about this during her Kind Leader interview. Pennie said, "I constantly remind myself, and others, that as a leader, you need to say many more kind things than negative things. That's because kind words slide off like Teflon, and negative ones stick like Velcro".[17] Thinking back to what you learned about negativity bias in Chapter 4, this makes total sense.

So, how can you, as a Kind Leader, practice refraining from speaking unkindly? When I was growing up, I remember my mother saying, "If you don't have anything nice to say, don't say anything at all".[18] It's a phrase that goes through my head whenever I'm in a situation in which I feel that my words and how I say them, might be perceived as unkind by those I am speaking with. When I hear the phrase running through my mind, it's a cue for me to stop and check my thoughts. As a leader, figuring out a way to know when to speak up, and when to stay silent, is extremely important. Here are some suggestions about how to go about it:

- *Pay attention to emotional cues*. Before anything else, a leader is a human being. Because human beings are more likely to say unkind things in unkind ways when they are frustrated, upset and angry, it's important to understand and pay attention to your emotional cues. Know what situations make you upset and monitor yourself carefully in those situations.
- *Create a catchphrase to catch yourself.* Just like I hear my mother's voice in my head, you can create a catchphrase to catch yourself. When you hear that phrase in your head, you'll know that you need to stop and consider whether it's a time to speak, or a time to stay silent.
- *Call a time out*. As a leader, you need to actively model kind behavior for your followers. Choosing to stop and think and making a conscious decision not to speak unkindly is a behavior you want others to have as well. Calling a time out (including using a hand-signal) is a great way to signal that your words aren't going to be as kind as you'd like and you need to take time out to stop, think, reflect and reword.

Practicing *If it's not kind, don't say it*, may take you a little time, but it will be well worth it, and goes a long way toward creating a culture of trust. As Ann Howell, leadership coach and consultant says, "An act of kindness can be choosing *not to* do something that isn't kind. *Not to* say something that isn't kind. Leaving the room if you feel that you can't not be judgmental is still an action".[19]

Before finishing this section, I'd like to leave you with one last thing to think about. A little while ago, while scrolling through social media I came across a discussion about how the idea of *politically correct* ('PC'), was infringing on people's ability to say what they would like to. In fact, the article even referenced the 'sticks and stones' saying that I talked about, explaining that parents used it to teach children so that they could learn that ultimately, they were responsible for their own feelings and emotions, not others: "We understood that people might have a bad opinion of us, and they might even say bad things about us, but their words could only hurt us if we let them".[20] In many organizations the idea of 'politically correct', that certain words and phrases aren't (or are) to be used, has become highly contested and heatedly debated. Should people be required to use certain terms and not use others? What about different types of pronouns? What about stating unpopular views? From the Kind Leader point of view, it's the leader's job to make sure that everyone in the organization feels comfortable and safe with the words and terms being used. Kind Leaders *consider others first*, so if there are words and phrases that make others uncomfortable and afraid, they should not be used. That's not 'politically correct'. It's simply kind.

Kind Leaders Practice the Basics: Say Please, Thank You and I'm Sorry

Now that you've learned about the three key Speak Kindly behaviors, *Choose your words kindly*, *Use a kind tone of voice* and *If it's not kind, don't say it*, I'd like to remind you about some other basic, kind behaviors that as a leader, you should be modeling. Those are saying please, thank you and I'm sorry. Although they might seem too basic, after the other Speak Kindly behaviors discussed in this chapter, they're simple key behaviors that leaders need to practice each and every day. When you ask someone to do something for you, as leaders do so often, please say 'please'. Asking politely doesn't imply weakness or that you aren't serious, it's kind. And it models how you expect others to treat each other. When someone completes a task, to your liking or not, or gives you something, please say thank you! It shows that instead of being focused on you, and what you are getting, you are considering others, and the time and effort they are putting in. And when you are wrong, apologize. No one, including you, is perfect. We all make mistakes. As you saw in Chapter 3, when I apologized to Lili, she immediately apologized to the other Director. Saying please, thank you and I'm sorry are three basic phrases that go a long way to creating a kind culture.

Speaking Kindly Ties Thoughts to Actions

Speaking Kindly is the Kind Leader Practice that links Kind Leaders' thoughts to actions. The more you speak kindly, the more you'll find that your thoughts are kinder as well. And, as you will 'see' in the next chapter, speaking kindly will help you to act in kinder ways too, because, as I always say, "Our words influence our actions and create the world around us".[21] Now, if you haven't done the exercises already, it's time to get started practicing the three Key Speak Kindly behaviors.

Practice: Practical Exercises to Use to Turn Your Thoughts into Action

How conscious are you of the words that you speak? What about those you write in emails? Do your words incite fear, or do they inspire trust? In individual followers and throughout the organization? What about your tone of voice and body language? Do you know when to speak and when it's kinder not to? As you saw, Speaking Kindly requires you to be conscious and deliberate in what words you choose to use and body language habits. Pay attention to how you speak and ask others to help you see and hear words, phrases and nonverbal cues that are unkindly creating fearful relationships. When you 'see' them, replace them with words, tone and body language that models kindness and creates a culture of trust. And please: practice, practice, practice!

Exercise 1: Becoming Conscious of Your Words

Before you can deliberately choose your words kindly, you'll need to become conscious of the words you currently use. Both in speaking and in writing. Ask two people who know you well to tell you words that they often hear you use. Are you surprised by what they said? Why or why not?

Becoming conscious of the words you currently use

To become conscious of the words that you use on a regular basis, ask at least two people who are close to you to tell you words that they often hear you use. Then check your email to see what common words run through them. Note them here.

Words people hear me use commonly	Words I often use in emails

Figure 5.3 Practice consciously changing unkind words to kind ones.

Exercise 2: Deliberately Replacing Unkind Words with Kind Ones

Now that you know what words you commonly use in speaking and writing, you can decide if their denotative and connotative meanings are as kind as you'd like them to be. Are they human? Living? Organic? Do they elicit trust? Focus on the means? If not, what others could you replace them with? Use a dictionary or thesaurus to help if needed.

Are your words kind? If not, what words will you replace them with?

Use the words from the list you created in Exercise 1. Write out their denotative and connotative meanings. Decide if they are kind words that you want to keep using. Note that in the 'Keep or Replace' column. In the last column, write the new words that you will replace unkind ones with.

Word	Denotative meaning	Connotative meaning	Keep or replace	Word/phrase to use instead

Figure 5.4 Deliberately replace unkind words with kind ones.

Exercise 3: Is Your Body Language Kind or Not?

Being deliberate about word choice is only one part of speaking kindly. To better understand your body language habits, ask a couple of close friends to point out body language habits you have and whether they perceive them as kind or not. Decide what to replace unkind ones with and practice the new, kind ones in front of a mirror until you feel comfortable with them.

What's your body language saying? Is it kind or not?

Ask friends and family to point out body language habits you might not be conscious of and if they are perceived as kind or not. Note the reasons. Then choose kind body language to replace the unkind body language. Practice until you are comfortable.

Current body language habit	Perceived as kind or unkind? Why?	Body language to replace with

Figure 5.5 Deliberately replace unkind body language with kind body language.

Exercise 4: Deliberately Replacing Unkind Words with Kind Ones

Having a kind tone of voice is the third part of speaking kindly. Record yourself in a variety of situations. Put on your Follower Hat and listen and play back the recording. Listen for breath, volume, speed and pitch in each of the situations. Is your tone of voice kind or not? What do you need to change to make it kinder?

How's your tone of voice? Is it kind or not? Record yourself in the situations listed below. Listen to your tone of voice for breath, volume, speed and pitch. Would your tone of voice be perceived as kind or unkind? How could you change your tone of voice to a kinder one? Record your practices and play them for others. Ask what they think.		
Current tone of voice	**Perceived as kind or unkind? Why?**	**Tone to replace with**
When I am calm: Breath Volume Speed Pitch		
When I am tired: Breath Volume Speed Pitch		
When I am angry: Breath Volume Speed Pitch		
In email: Breath Volume Speed Pitch		

Figure 5.6 Deliberately replace unkind tone of voice with a with kind one.

Reflection: What Would You Do? Kind Leader Practice Scenarios

Now that you've had the opportunity to read the ideas and theory presented in the Discussion section and do the Practice exercises, it's time to reflect on what you've learned and proactively plan how to apply those learnings.

I'm sure you are wondering how Kay'La Janson and Kevin Landrell are doing as they continue on their journey to lead kindly. Let's check in and see.

Practice Speaking Kindly Because Your Words Create Your Followers' World

Scenario 1 – Kay'La's Story: If You Use 'Fighting Words' Don't Be Surprised If You Get a Fight!

Kay'La Janson picked up the paper and read the words in the email that Anderson has printed out and put on her desk. Then she put the paper down, got up, walked over to the window and stared out, deep in reflection. She was back at home office, having spent the past few weeks traveling the 'Codstom world', visiting branches, meeting with leaders and 'walking the floor', getting to know the supervisors and service representatives who took care of Codstom's clients day after day. Kay'La had surprised quite a few people when she asked to spend some time at each branch listening in on calls, both to hear the actual voice of Codstom's customers, and also to hear how the 'voice of Codstom' sounded to them. And she'd been thinking about what she'd seen and heard ever since.

Kay'La went back to her desk, sat down and picked up the email again. It had been sent to her by Kevin Landrell, one of the supervisors that she had met in the past few weeks. Kevin said that he had quite a few complaints from customers about some of the words the service reps used, and their tone of voice. Kay'La had heard some examples herself while she listened in on calls, and as she'd listened to how managers talked to supervisors. She'd asked Kevin to keep in touch with her about the situation, and the email that she had asked Anderson to print was forwarded to her from Kevin. It was originally from Kevin's assistant branch manager, Cindy Yang, and had been sent to all the branch supervisors. "I'm sure that Cindy never thought it would reach me", Kay'La thought to herself. "Otherwise, she probably wouldn't have said those negative, unkind things about our clients and our service reps. Or threatened to 'cut heads' if results didn't improve. I'm sure the team there must feel worried and scared. If this is the way that management is talking, it's no wonder that the words and tone I heard service reps using is what it is. 'Fighting words' don't bring people together. They just separate them and cause more problems. I'm so glad I decided to do my 'world tour' and see and hear for myself. Now it's time for me to ..."

Now It's Your Turn to Reflect and Apply

Put on your Leader Hat and think about what you would do in this situation. Who would you start with? What would you choose to say, how would you say it, and what would you decide not to say? How would you 'speak' to the wider organization? Write your ideas here:

Scenario 2 – Kevin's Story: 'I Don't Want to Believe My Ears ...'

Kevin Landrell was feeling conflicted. On the one hand, he had been super-excited that the CEO, Kay'La Janson had chosen to spend time talking directly with him and listening to his team members serve customers. What an honor! Kevin had never worked in any organization where any senior leader had even walked through a service area, let alone spent time talking with supervisors, service reps and listening in on calls. It was refreshing and exciting! It was also nerve-wracking, though, because despite Kevin's best efforts to improve the language and tone of voice his team members used, he hadn't made as much progress as he would have liked to.

"It's an uphill battle", Kevin thought to himself. "Even though we've spent a lot of time together as a team talking about what words are okay to use, and what words aren't, I still hear people talking to each other and to customers unkindly. And it's worse if they are tired, frustrated or if the customer isn't happy. Especially Molly. Sitting beside Jaden has been a good influence on her, but she still loses her temper and bad-mouth's customers too often."

As Kevin was contemplating the situation, Cindy Yang, the assistant branch manager walked by on her way back from the staff lounge. She was carrying a coffee in one hand and holding her cell phone to her ear with the other. Suddenly, Cindy let out a long list of expletives. As Kevin and the team turned around, they could see she had spilled her hot coffee. "Guess what you've made me do now? Spill hot coffee all over myself. You and your stupid mistakes. If you weren't so incompetent, we'd have more sales. And fewer complaints from home office", Cindy barked into the phone. Dumping her now empty coffee cup into the garbage pail beside Molly's desk, Cindy finished her conversation by growling, "I'll see you in my office in thirty minutes, and you better come prepared with a plan to get us out of this mess, or there will be some pretty severe consequences". Hanging up the phone, Cindy made a slashing motion to her throat, and then stomped angrily off. Kevin looked at the team. Molly was staring intently at Cindy. "If it's okay for her to say those things, why can't we? She is the 'big boss' after all", Molly said mockingly to Kevin and the rest of team.

Kevin stood up, faced Molly and the team and …

Now It's Your Turn to Reflect and Apply

Put on your Leader Hat. Have you ever been in a situation like this? What did you do then? What would you do now, knowing what you do about the three key Speak Kindly behaviors? What would you say to Molly and the team? How would you say it? And what should Kevin do about Cindy Yang? Write about what you would do here:

Chapter 5 Kind-Points

- *The Three Key Speak Kindly Behaviors are Choose Your Words Kindly, Use a Kind Tone of Voice and If it's Not Kind, Don't Say it!* The three key behaviors are interconnected and flow from each other. Speaking kindly is also the practice that links Thinking Kindly with Acting Kindly. Your words come from your thoughts and generate actions.
- *Choose Your Words Kindly.* As a leader you need to consciously choose words that have denotative and connotative meanings that are kind. The words you use will travel fast, far and have a huge influence on individual followers and the type of culture that is created. Unkind words create a culture of fear. Kind words create a culture of trust.
- *Use a Kind Tone of Voice.* Leaders speak often and the meaning of their words isn't just conveyed by the word itself. Body language and tone of voice convey over 90 percent of meaning and weigh more heavily than word choice in situations where emotion and feeling is involved. Kind Leaders are conscious of modeling kind body language and tone of voice.
- *If It's Not Nice, Don't Say It.* Kind Leaders know that knowing when not to speak at all is just as important as choosing words, body language and tone of voice consciously and deliberately. Taking time to stop and think, especially when you are frustrated, upset and angry will help you speak more kindly when you do.
- *Kind Leaders Remember the Basics: Please, Thank You and I'm Sorry.* Kind words like please, thank you and I'm sorry go a long way toward creating relationships with individual followers and model the basics of communication of a kind culture. People aren't numbers, and they aren't 'ends'. Modeling basic politeness and kindness helps keep focus on the means.

Notes

1 Jamie Flinchbaugh quote on my LinkedIn Post on October 12, 2020.
2 https://cmoe.com/blog/do-you-spend-80-of-your-time-communicating/ downloaded December 26, 2020. Center for Management and Organization Effectiveness.
3 Personal conversation with Michelle Jorgensen in 2018. Reiterated during a personal interview on November 5, 2020.
4 Personal conversation with Michelle Jorgensen in 2018.
5 Connotative Words: Examples and Exercises, https://examples.yourdictionary.com/examples-of-connotative-words.html Downloaded on December 29, 2020.
6 Women in Lean – Our Table is a collaborative group of women continuous improvement practitioners working to raise the voices of women in the field. You can learn more at www.womeninlean.org
7 Personal conversation with Michelle Hlywa on December 10, 2020.
8 Personal conversation with Michelle Jorgensen in 2018.
9 Is Nonverbal Communication a Numbers Game? Jeff Thompson, PhD, www.psychologytoday.com/us/blog/beyond-words/201109/is-nonverbal-communication-numbers-gameDownloaded on December 29, 2020.
10 Ibid.
11 Carol Kinsey Gorman, Busting 5 Body Language Myths www.forbes.com/sites/carolkinseygoman/2012/07/24/busting-5-body-language-myths/?sh=26614c273922 Downloaded December 30, 2020.
12 Ibid.
13 Personal conversation with Doug Wotherspoon on December 31, 2020.
14 What Does Your Voice Convey? https://exploringyourmind.com/what-does-your-tone-of-voice-convey/ Downloaded December 31, 2020.
15 Maria Pellicano, Improve Your Tone of Voice to Communicate More Effectively, https://theladiescoach.com/passion-and-purpose/improve-your-tone-of-voice-to-communicate-more-effectively/ Downloaded December 31, 2020.
16 Personal Interview with Kathi Littman on December 24, 2020.
17 Personal Interview with Pennie Saum on January 23, 2020.
18 Pamela Ross, author's mother. In many instances throughout the author's childhood!
19 Personal interview with Ann Howell on October 17, 2020.
20 Leslyn Lewis, A Strong Society Must Encourage, Not Limit, Debate https://nationalpost.com/opinion/leslyn-lewis-a-strong-society-must-encourage-not-limit-debate Downloaded on October 12, 2020.
21 Karyn Ross, *Think Kindy – Speak Kindly – Act Kindly: 366 Easy and Free Ideas You Can Use to Create a Kinder World … Starting Today*, The Love and Kindness Project Foundation, 2020, p. 68.

Chapter 6

Act Kindly

Kind Leaders Put Humanity First

We may be making machines, but the people who work for us aren't machines.
Stewart Bellamy, Manufacturing sector leader

Discussion: Kind Leaders Lead by Kind Example

Before discussing the Third Key Kind Leader Practice, Act Kindly, I'd like you to think back to two definitions that you learned in Chapter 1. The first is the definition of a follower: A follower is a person who has decided to pay attention to, take their cues about how to act and react, and have their thoughts, words and actions influenced by, a person they deem as 'leader'.

Second, is the definition of kindness: Kindness is an action (or set of actions), connecting a person's internal feelings of empathy and compassion to others that is undertaken with the purpose of generating a positive effect and outcome for another.

As you can see, both definitions have the word *action* in them. That's because thinking about leading with kindness and speaking about it isn't enough. Leading with kindness requires action. It requires leading by example, and not just any example. It requires leading by kind example. According to the *Merriam-Webster* dictionary, the word example means

DOI: 10.4324/9781003141433-6

"one that serves as a pattern to be imitated or not to be imitated".[1] From the Kind Leader point of view, 'leading by kind example' means *purposefully acting and reacting with kindness to generate positive effects and outcomes for others*. Because leaders influence the thoughts, words and actions of their followers, who wear Leader Hats in many different situations and places, when Kind Leaders lead by kind example, instead of creating a vicious circle of unkindness like the one described in Chapter 3 (Figure 3.1 on page 40), their actions spread far and wide and create a world of kindness.

Acting Kindly Is the Third of The Three Key Kind Leader Practices

In this chapter, you'll learn about and practice the three key behaviors of the third Kind Leader Practice: *Act Kindly*. The Act Kindly behaviors are: *Check in with people, not on them; Listen: With open eyes, open ears, open mind and an open heart*, and *Recognize others*. Throughout this chapter you'll learn about how to practice the three key Act Kindly behaviors to form deep, lasting human connections and create trusting relationships. You'll also learn how to care for and nurture your people so that they grow and blossom in all areas of their life. Like the think Kindly and Speak Kindly behaviors, The Act Kindly behaviors are interconnected; they flow from and influence each other. The more you practice the Act Kindly behaviors the easier it will get to lead by kind example.

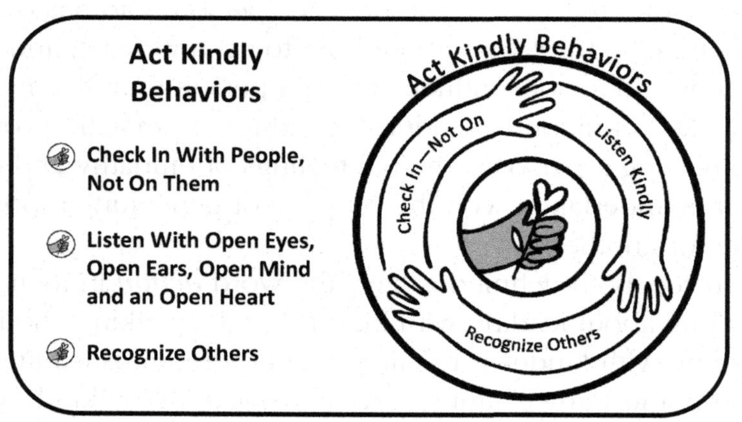

Figure 6.1 Act Kindly Behaviors.

Act Kindly Behavior 1: Check in with *People, Not on Them*

The first of the key Act Kindly Behaviors is *Check in with people, not on them*. As you learned in Chapter 5, *choosing your words kindly* is a key Kind Leader behavior. That's why I didn't call this behavior check in with '*employees* or *staff* or *workers*' or any of the other terms often used to describe followers. I deliberately chose to use the word *people*, because, before anything else, followers are people. Whole people. Not 'things'. Their functions and jobs don't define them, their humanity does. It's also why I chose the phrase check *in with* and not check *on*. In ends-focused results-oriented organizations, leaders check *on* employees to make sure they're doing what they're being paid to do. Because Kind Leaders focus on the means and *consider others first*, they *check in with people* to get to know them as people and to help them, just like Grace's leader did in Chapter 2. Jim Semple, a retired manufacturing Vice President, described this beautifully during his Kind Leader interview:

> As someone once said, "There are 'people' people and there are 'things' people." 'Things' people see workers as chess pieces to be managed and manipulated to serve their purposes. These people tend to be autocratic leaders who may be effective in their own way, but who do not create a workplace where people thrive and enjoy their work. 'Things' people see kindness as weakness. Workers may stay in order to earn a paycheck, and nothing more. 'People' people like and care about others and have the personality and character that qualifies them to be effective leaders. Kindness and empathy are in their nature. Employees 'feel the love' and will go to great lengths to not disappoint their boss.[2]

Checking in with people helps leaders become people 'people' in two ways. First it allows them to get to know and care about those who work for them as whole *people*, and second, it ensures they are spending the time they need to see how their people are feeling, how they are doing, and what help they need.

Get to Know Your People as People

As I did the interviews for this book, I started to notice something. When I asked people to tell me about a specific time a leader was kind to them, almost all of the stories were about things their leader did that crossed over into their personal life. Amir Ghannad, whom you met in previous chapters, told me about how his manager treated him when his wife and daughter were in a near fatal car crash. Amir had just arrived in New Jersey that morning when he was notified about the accident in Atlanta. Looking at Amir's face, his leader could tell something was wrong even though Amir was still in shock and still trying to take the situation in. When his leader heard what happened, he told Amir to go back to Atlanta, arranged for him to be driven to the airport and had Amir's plane ticket booked for him. Amir's leader also let Amir know that he could take as much time off as he wanted and needed and then his leader *checked in* frequently to see how Amir and his family were feeling. As you can imagine, Amir didn't just feel like a valued 'employee', he felt deeply cared about and cared for as a person.[3]

Stewart Bellamy, another manufacturing sector leader, told me about how Sanjay, a Vice President, treated him after Stewart's younger brother died. Sanjay arranged to have Stewart's whole team attend the memorial service with him. And Sanjay did as well. Reflecting back on how much of an impact Sanjay's kindness had at the time (and years later as he told me this story), Stewart said:

> A leader is aware of what is happening in a person's *life*, not just at work. I don't believe that the line should be work/life balance. Work is part of life. The relationship doesn't exist between work and life, but between *people* and *people*, whether at work or in other things we do as part of our life.[4]

Many years ago when I worked at the very ends-focused organization where 'the number was the number', leadership firmly directed the staff to 'leave your personal life' at home. 'Employees' were expected to be 'trained professionals' at all times and not bring their 'feelings' to work. The problem with this was that it was a customer service job. Empathy, compassion and kindness were important qualities needed to create deep, trusting relationships with customers and between leadership and the people doing the work.

Kind Leaders know that in order to get to know your people as *people* and develop a culture of trust, you can't ask them to leave their 'personal lives' and feelings at home. As Cheryl Jensen, the Higher Education leader you met in Chapter 1 who walked the halls of her organization *checking in with* each person she met, says:

> Leadership is about valuing people for who they are as people. If people don't feel valued by their leader as whole people, they will feel broken, unseen and uncared for. And if that is how they feel, how will they be inspired to greatness?[5]

KLC Stop & Think Point Put on your Leader Hat and think about how you feel when your followers tell you about their personal lives and/or express emotions and feelings. Do you encourage your followers to be whole people, or are you asking them to leave part of themselves at home?

Now it's time to put on your Leader Hat and think about how well you know your people as people. To find out, go to this chapter's Practice Section and complete the exercise (Figure 6.3) on page 130. (You can stop and do the exercise now or continue reading and do it at the end of this chapter.)

Kind Leaders Spend Their Time Checking in with People

Getting to know your people as whole people is an important part of the first key Act Kindly behavior, but it's only the first part. The second part is actually spending time with them, so that you get to know *how* they're feeling and *how* they're doing. So you can help them. As you saw in Chapter 3, 'leaving people alone to do their work' isn't the way to help them learn and grow. And it's not the way to show them you truly care for them as people either. Spending your time *checking in with* them is.

In many organizations, followers don't see their leaders very often or spend very much time with them at all. In a 2014 study of more than 33,000 executives, managers and employees undertaken by Leadership IQ, almost half of the participants reported spending three or fewer hours each week interacting with their leader, and 20 percent of those surveyed spent just one hour a week.[6] That's only a little more than thirty minutes a day on the high end, and twelve minutes a day on the low end.

How much time does your leader spend with you? Put on your Follower Hat and think about it. Is it every day? During a weekly team meeting? Only if there is a crisis or if they need you to do something? Or maybe you don't spend time with your leader at all. Next, keeping your Follower Hat on, now think about what happens when you do spend time with your leader. Do they ask about how you are feeling? About what's happening in your life? Do they know the names of your family members and ask about them? Or is it 'strictly business' with your leader 'checking on' the progress you've made on the work you've been assigned?

Jim Semple told me a great story about how he *checked in with people* in his job as Vice President of a manufacturing company. Jim said:

> I spent the first hour or two every morning walking through our large plant chatting with employees. The conversations touched on work and personal topics. I took an interest in the personal and family life of employees. Having been a shop floor worker in my early days, I realized the huge effect one's family life has on job performance. I also remembered the uplifting feeling I had when the owner actually stopped by my work bench to ask, 'How are you doing Jimmie?' While doing my daily walk-around I didn't consider it an act of kindness. I was genuinely interested in our workers as people – mothers, fathers, sons, daughters, etc.[7]

As Vice President of the plant, Jim didn't walk the floor each morning to 'check on' employees to make sure that they were doing *what* they were supposed to be doing. He walked the floor and *checked in with* people because he cared about *how* they were feeling as and *how* they were doing.

Checking in with people enables leaders to lead by kind example and purposefully act and react with kindness to generate positive effects and outcomes for others. Remember, over 90 percent of communication comes from body language and tone of voice. If leaders don't actually 'see and hear' the people they are leading, they won't know how those people are feeling, and doing. Because Stewart Bellamy *checked in with* his people, he knew what to do when he found out that a new member of his quality assurance team would be alone for the holidays:

The team member had just relocated to the city to take on the position and didn't know anyone here. So, my wife and I invited them to join us for a meal during their first Christmas break. We were subsequently invited to join them in celebration at their Hindu Temple when their first child was born.[8]

KLC Stop & Think Point How deliberate are you in how you act and react to the needs of your people? Put on your Leader Hat and think about what you've done in past when one of your people has been in need. Was it deliberately kind? What could you have done differently? What will you do next time?

So, here's the question: How much time should you spend *checking in with* your people? The answer: As much time as *you* need to be able to understand what you need to do to kindly help them. And, as much time as *they* need from you to grow and blossom as whole people! The Leadership IQ study quoted above found that people "who spent six or more hours a week (more than an hour a day, for a five day work week) with their leader rather than only one hour, were twenty-nine percent more inspired, thirty percent more engaged, sixteen percent more innovative and fifteen percent more intrinsically motivated".[9]

As a leader, people know that your time is precious. When you spend that time *checking in* with them, they understand how precious they are to you because of who they are as people, not just because of what they do. If you don't spend as much time as you should *checking in with* your people, here are some ideas about how to get started and what to do:

- *Put your people first.* Before you do anything else in your day (check your email, look at reports, meet with *your* leader), spend time checking in with your people. Whether it's walking the shop floor like Jim Semple did, or checking in virtually, like Petrina McGrath (who you met in Chapter 2) does, make checking in with your people your very first priority, every single day. Schedule it on your calendar and theirs and leave your devices behind so you can give your people your undivided attention.

- *Be with your people.* One of the best ways to check in with people is to make sure that you are located where you can see and hear them easily, and they can see and hear you easily. If you aren't currently co-located, move. Cheryl Jensen moved from her fifth-floor corner office to a glass-walled office in high-traffic area on the main floor where she could see and *check in with people* easily. If you lead people in different locations, rotate where you work from. Go to where your people are and spend time with them there. And once you're there, make sure you're not away in meetings all day.
- *Ask open-ended questions.* To get to know your people as people ask open-ended questions like "How are you feeling today?", "What's going on in your life?" and "How is your family doing?" Learn the names of your people's family members and pets. Find out what your people love to do outside of work. And what they are struggling with. Then ask questions like "How can I help?" and "What do you need to make progress?" Open-ended questions are those that don't have just a 'yes' or 'no' answer. By asking people open-ended questions, you will be able to learn more about them as people and about how you can help them.
- *Listen.* As you saw in Chapter 5, leaders spend an awful lot of time speaking. To get to know your people as people, and to be able to deliberately decide how to act and react kindly to their needs, instead of talking, you are going to have to listen to them. With open eyes, open ears, open mind and an open heart. To their feelings, emotions and needs as whole people. You'll learn more about how to do this in the next Act Kindly key behavior.

Earlier in this chapter, I asked you to put on your Follower Hat and think about how much time you spent with your leader. It probably was easy for you to do. Now I'm going to ask you to put on your Leader Hat and think about how much time you actually spend with your followers. If you're like many leaders, you might not know. Leaders have a lot to do in their day and a lot of 'things' to spend their time on. To help you see where you're currently spending your time, and how much of it is with your people, go to this chapter's Practice Section and complete the exercise (Figure 6.4) on page 131. (You can stop and do the exercise now or continue reading and do it at the end of this chapter.)

Checking in with People Creates a Culture of Trust

Before discussing the second key Act Kindly behavior, *Listen: With open eyes, open ears, open mind and an open heart*, I'd like to address something that may be making some of you uncomfortable: the common idea that leaders need to wait until people trust them before asking about their personal lives. At this point, you may be thinking to yourself, "Don't you have to build trust with people first? What if they are having problems that they don't want you to know about? What if they don't want to share their feelings and emotions? And if I *check in with people* often, won't they think I'm micromanaging them?" Because you may have worked (or still work) in an organization that has a culture of fear, this may be your 'go to' way of thinking.

Kind Leaders know that the best way to create trusting relationships and to build a culture of trust is to spend time getting to know people as people. That way, as leaders, they can purposefully act and react quickly and kindly to the very human problems their people have. *Checking in with people* isn't about micromanaging them and the work that they're doing like checking on people is. *Checking in with* people is about caring for them as whole people and precious human beings. So, if you're worried that it's too soon to ask people about how they're feeling and how they're doing, please stop waiting and get started. As I always say, "*Don't wait for people to trust you to ask them about their lives. Ask them and get to know them, and then they will trust you*".

Act Kindly Behavior 2 – Listen: With Open Eyes, Open Ears, Open Mind and an Open Heart

The second key Act Kindly behavior is *Listen: With open eyes, open ears, open mind and an open heart.* It's a key behavior first, because in order for leaders to really know how their people are feeling and doing, they need to listen with open eyes and open ears. Second, in order to truly hear what their followers need, leaders need to listen with an open mind and an open heart.

To get started, I have a couple of questions for you. Please put on your Leader Hat and think about how much of your leadership development time has been spent focused on improving your speaking ability. Maybe you've taken formal training courses or been part of a public speaking club. Maybe you've even had a dedicated speech coach. Now think about how much time you've devoted to improving your listening skills. I'm going to guess that there's a huge discrepancy. Maybe you're one of the lucky ones whose organization has some type of online in-house training on listening, but if you you're like most people I know, you probably haven't had any formal training at all. You might not even have thought about listening as a leadership skill that can, and should, be improved. And that's a problem, because out of the 80 percent of their day leaders spend communicating, about 45 percent of the time isn't spent on speaking. It's spent on listening. And most people just aren't very good listeners.[10]

Why aren't people, and leaders, good listeners? In an article on listening skills, Dick Lee and Delmar Hatesohl suggest a number of reasons. The first is people's ability to think much faster than they can speak. Because of this discrepancy, people only use about 25 percent of their mental capacity while listening so their minds tend to wander off. Additionally, people aren't efficient listeners. People only retain about 50 percent of what they hear initially, and after 48 hours, that drops to about 25 percent. Other problems include deterioration of listening skills with age, and the amount of energy it takes to really listen.[11] Because leaders are people first, they are subject to all of these common listening problems.

As well as the above, there is another reason why leaders struggle with listening. And that reason is particularly pertinent to kind leadership. As you saw in Chapter 5, leaders tend to spend a lot of time speaking *to* their followers: they give directives and have the final 'say' in what happens. That's because in many traditional models of leadership leaders aren't focused on others as people. They're 'things' people, focused on the ends and on bottom line results. If leaders only see their followers as 'things' why would they need to listen to them? Followers are just there to get the job done and to listen to what leaders have to say to them, not to be heard from.

KLC Stop & Think Point How much time do you spend deeply listening to your people? With your Leader Hat on, take a moment to reflect on it. If you aren't spending much time, or listening deeply, what does that tell you about whether your people see you as a 'things' person or a 'people' person?

Kind Leaders aren't 'things' people, though, they're 'people' people. And in order to hear what those people need Kind Leaders need to listen. Actively. In an Entrepreneur.com article on the importance of listening as a leadership skill, Stacey Hanke says, "Active listening demonstrates concern for others, and fosters cohesive bonds, commitment and trust. It can reduce the frequency of interpersonal conflict while increasing the odds of a quick resolution when conflicts should arise. A study published in *The International Journal of Listening* concluded that "listening is considered to be the single most important communication skill necessary, even valued more highly than speaking, for leaders in the business world".[12] For Kind Leaders, actively listening means listening with open eyes, open ears, open mind and an open heart. And it's a practice that needs to be practiced often. Here's how to do it:

Listen with Open Eyes

You may be wondering why *listening with open eyes* is the first part of how Kind Leaders practice listening. Isn't listening something people do with their ears? The answer is, only partly. As you learned above, one of the common problems most people have with listening is that their auditory processing is very inefficient. People don't remember much of what they hear with their ears. Coupled with this is the fact that such a large percentage of spoken meaning isn't communicated through the actual words used, but through body language.

To *listen with open eyes*, you need to be able to physically see the person you are speaking with. If you can be in the same location, the best way to *listen with open eyes* is to go to where the person you are listening to does their work. Often, leaders ask followers to come to them, instead of going to where their follower is. For leaders, that is a barrier to being able to really 'see' how the person you're speaking with is doing, because the person is out of their element. If they come to your office, you won't be able to see what their surroundings are like. And if there is a big difference in hierarchical power, the person might feel uncomfortable in your space . . . like they are being sent to the principal's office!

If you can't physically be with the person, video chat platforms, with cameras turned on, are the next best thing. For leaders, COVID-19 has actually been a great opportunity to 'see' their people as whole people. There's no way to ask people to 'leave their personal life at home' when they are working from home. I'm often surprised when leaders tell me that they don't ask people to turn on their video while they are working from home because they think their followers might be reluctant to do so. As a leader, I'd have to ask myself why I think people might be reluctant to turn their camera on. Are they afraid that someone (their leader) is going to judge their surroundings? That children are going to come into the picture? Or that a dog might bark during a meeting? Those concerns can be evidence of a culture of fear, where people don't feel like they can bring their 'whole self' to work. And what happens if you see something on camera that worries you, or if you notice that the person you're chatting with seems to be in want or need? As a leader, you then have a wonderful opportunity to act and react kindly to help the person.

Whether in person, or by video chat, during your conversation, look directly at the person you are speaking with. Make eye contact and watch their body language. Is there a discrepancy between what their words and body language are saying? Do they look stressed, even though they 'say' they are fine? Are their arms crossed? Maybe they aren't really 'open' to what you are saying, even though they say they are. What about their facial expressions? Are they smiling, frowning or furrowing their brow? All of these are clues to how the person you are speaking with is feeling. Clues, that if you don't *listen with open eyes,* are easy to miss. Because so much of communication is carried through body language, paying close attention to what you are 'seeing' will help you accurately hear what the person is really saying.

If you're reading this and saying to yourself, "This doesn't apply to me … most of the communication I have with my employees is by email or text", I'm going to ask you to reconsider. You can't 'see' how someone is feeling from reading an email. And 'reading between the lines' can cause you to make a lot of assumptions and jump to inaccurate conclusions and decisions. Expressions like 'seeing is believing' and 'I won't believe it until I see it with my own eyes' all show the importance of *listening with open eyes.* As a leader, when you *listen with open eyes*, you'll make fewer assumptions because you've seen for yourself, and the people you are speaking with will feel 'seen' as well as heard.

Listen with Open Ears

For Kind Leaders, *listening with open ears* means paying attention to the words that people are using and to their tone of voice as well. As you learned in Chapter 5, words have *denotative* and *connotative* meanings.

Their denotative meanings are the literal ones from the dictionary, while their connotative meanings convey the word's emotional undertones, feelings and other associations. *Listening with open ears* means paying attention to both types of meaning. As well, leaders need to listen to the speaker's tone of voice: breath, volume, speed and pitch.

Although *listening with open ears* would seem self-explanatory (after all, it is what most people think listening is all about), it's not as easy as it sounds. First, a quiet environment is necessary. If there is a lot of noise, it will be hard to hear word choice and tone of voice. Also, because leaders tend to have a lot on their mind, quiet environments have less distractions, making it easier to for them to pay attention to the person they are listening to. Like *listening with open eyes*, *listening with open ears* works better when the leader and the person they are listening to are in the same place and can see each other. Choose a quiet room, or a video chat platform that has a clear connection.

Once everyone's settled, the first step to *listening with open ears* is to pay careful attention to the words that the person you are listening to chooses to use. What are their denotative meanings and do the connotative meanings and tone of voice match the denotative meanings? Listen carefully as those will give you clues to how the person really feels and what they really mean. For example, in response to a question about how they are feeling about being moved to another team, the person you are listening to might answer, "I'm fine. Really just fine". At first sound, it might seem like they are okay with the decision. However, their tone of voice might be sharp and sarcastic, or the pitch might be low and sad. Coupled with the fact that the connotative meaning of the word 'fine' can be 'not fine', as their leader, you have a clue that you should ask more open-ended questions and dig a little deeper. Your people shouldn't have to shout at you to get their message across. As a Kind Leader, it's up to *you to listen with open ears* to really hear what they have to say.

Keep Your Ears Pricked for Signals of Culture of Fear and Unkindness

As you learned in Chapter 5, leaders need to choose their words kindly because the words they use will be the words followers see as acceptable to use. As a leader, *listening with open ears* also means listening for whether the words followers are using are kind ones. Are they the kind words that, as a leader, you've chosen and are actively modeling? If not, then you'll need to spend some time reflecting on why they aren't. As you saw in Michelle's story in Chapter 5, Michelle's team members spoke about their coworkers the way Michelle spoke about them. Are you actively modeling the words you want your followers to use, or have you slipped back into old unkind word choice habits? Are unkind words from other places being imported into your culture? If they are, where did they come from, and what are you going to do?

And what about tone of voice? Are people shouting at each other or customers? Are they using other disrespectful tones such as sarcasm? Remember, followers wear Leader Hats in other cultures and may bring unacceptable words and tones of voice into yours.

As a Kind Leader *listening with open ears* is vital because the words and tone of voice that you hear convey critical information about your culture, including whether it is one of fear, or if it's one of kindness. You need to listen carefully, and if the words you're hearing aren't kind and express a culture of fear, as the leader, you need to do something. That's why *checking in with people* and *listening with open eyes, open ears* (and open and mind and open heart as you'll see shortly) isn't just the best way to see and hear how they are doing, it's also the best way to see and hear how your organization's culture is doing.

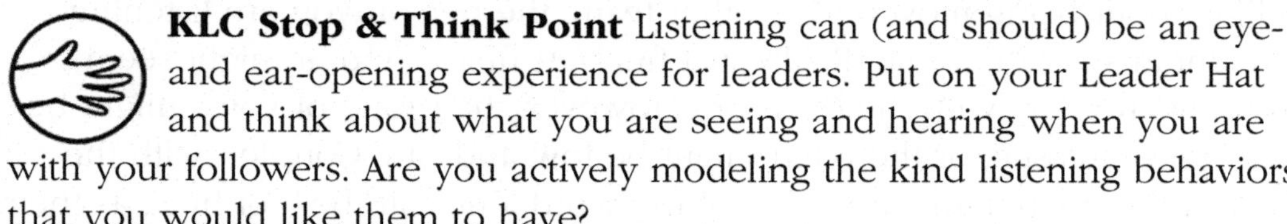

KLC Stop & Think Point Listening can (and should) be an eye- and ear-opening experience for leaders. Put on your Leader Hat and think about what you are seeing and hearing when you are with your followers. Are you actively modeling the kind listening behaviors that you would like them to have?

Listen with an Open Mind

You're probably familiar with the saying, 'People tend to hear only what they want to hear'. It turns out that it's true and there are two reasons why. The first is confirmation bias and the second is selective attention. Confirmation bias is the tendency for people to give more weight to information or evidence that confirms their already existing beliefs. It's effect is amplified for issues that have a strongly charged emotional component.[13] Selective attention means that because there is so much information bombarding us at all times, people only pay attention to some of it. Due to confirmation bias, that 'some of it' tends to be the things that confirm what people already believe.[14] These two factors make listening with an open mind difficult for people in general, and it can be especially difficult for leaders if they are ends-focused and emotionally tied to results.

For Kind Leaders, practicing *listening with an open mind* is the key to developing trust. People need to feel that they can tell their leaders what's happening from their perspective as *people*, and that their leader will *listen with an open mind* to what they are saying. Put on your Follower Hat and think back to a time that you told a leader something you thought they might not want to hear. Maybe, you were struggling to do the best you could but didn't have the training or resources you needed, like Grace, in Chapter 2. When you shared how you were feeling with your leader, how did they react? Did they *listen with an open mind* and offer to help as Grace's leader did? Or did they gloss over your concerns, tell you that your perspective was wrong and that no change was needed? Depending on what happened, I'm sure you felt very differently. If, as in Grace's case, you felt heard, and that your leader had an open mind, a trusting relationship probably developed. If not, and you felt that your words fell on 'deaf ears' you probably felt discouraged, unvalued, unseen and uncared for as Cheryl Jensen described above.

Because confirmation bias and selective attention make it easier to be closed-minded than open-minded, *listening with an open mind* is a deliberate choice Kind Leaders have to make each time they enter a conversation. And it's a skill they need to consciously practice. Frequently! Here's some suggestions about how you can practice:

- *Fully focus on what the other person is saying.* Notice when you are paying attention to the 'voice inside your head' instead of the voice of the person you are listening to. When you feel your attention slipping away, consciously silence your inner voice and turn your attention back to the person you are listening to.
- *Listen to 'hear' rather than to 'respond'.* In traditional models, leaders are often expected to have all the answers and to have them quickly. That makes them particularly susceptible to 'listening to respond' – deciding what to say next – rather than to listening to hear what the other person is saying. For a leader, this can be especially difficult if the person you are listening to says something you disagree with. To

listen to 'hear', let the person finish what they are saying before you start to think about how to respond. It's okay to say, 'Let me take a minute to think about what you've just said', before you answer. In fact, it's a perfect opportunity for you to *check your thoughts frequently* and models a key Think Kindly behavior.

- *Know the words, phrases (both denotative and connotative), body language and tone of voice that provoke strong emotions for you.* When you hear and see them, remind yourself that you'll need to work harder to be open-minded because you feel emotional. It's okay to tell the person you're listening to that you need a break to calm your thoughts, think clearly and *listen with an open mind.* After all, before you are a leader, you're a person! Doing this also models the kind of behavior you want your people to have.

Once you've opened your mind to hear what your people are saying, (even if it's not something you want to hear), as a leader, you have to decide what to do with what the person has told you. How to act and react and how to lead by kind example. That's where *listening with an open heart* comes in.

Listen with an Open Heart

For Kind Leaders, *listening with an open heart* is directly related to seeing – and hearing – your people, not as 'things', but as whole 'people'. As people, (and not machines as Stewart Bellamy reminds us so eloquently in this chapter's opening quote), each has different opinions, beliefs, problems and imperfections. Each has their own views, their own ways of seeing the world, and their own struggles. For Kind Leaders, *listening with an open heart* means using empathy and compassion to hear and respond to the very human needs of your people. To help them. Even when you might not agree with their point of view, political or religious beliefs or way of handling a situation.

Listening with an open heart is both the most difficult kind of listening and also the part of listening that enables a leader to act and react kindly to lead by kind example. Many years ago I worked on a small four-person team. The person who sat next to me was often late for work or absent unexpectedly. When that happened, the others on our team had to cover. People were often angry about this, and at our team member, as they had to do extra work. One day, the person didn't come to work. And didn't return for two months. When he returned he told us that he had been suffering with a mental health condition. Many people in the office thought that he should have been fired. That he hadn't been a good worker or team member previously and that going forward, he wouldn't be able to care for customers properly and would be unreliable. Our leader disagreed. She reminded everyone that no one is perfect. That all people have challenges and difficulties to overcome and that what each of us needed to do was open our heart, be kind and help the person get back to work as best they could. And people did. Because our leader led by kind example, others followed.

As a Kind Leader, *when you check in with people* as people, and really *listen,* you will see and hear many things which you will automatically disagree with because your background is different, your experience is different and your views are different. When you *listen with an open heart,* instead of immediately disagreeing and judging, you will be able to hear the hopes and dreams and pain and needs of others. But hearing isn't enough. As a Kind Leader you need to act and react kindly. *Listening with an open heart* means *considering others first* (Kind Leader Characteristic 3) and having empathy and compassion for the person you are listening to. As a leader, unless you *listen with an open heart*, it will be easy to close your eyes and look away from the difficulties your people are having as people. Then, instead of focusing on the means (Kind Leader Characteristic 5), you might make decisions that treat your people not as 'people', but as 'things'.

Recently, I had a discussion with a client who was frustrated with one of his people, and with himself, because of his own reaction. "The problem", he said, "Is that I don't know how to open my heart. I just don't know how". *Listening with an open heart* isn't easy, but it's the 'heart' of kind leadership. Here are some suggestions and questions to help you practice:

- *Learn to recognize when you are closed-minded.* The first step to opening your heart is to recognize when your mind is closed. Pay attention to what situations you are most closed-minded in. When you are in those situations, *frequently check your thoughts and feelings.* Take time to reflect and think deeply about why you feel the way you do. Ask yourself, "What is causing me to be closed-minded?"
- *Ask yourself whether you are seeing the person you are listening to as a 'person'.* If you don't see the person as a 'person', a human being just like you, it will be easy to close your heart. The more you see the person as a 'person', with emotions and feelings just like yours,

the easier it will be for you to feel empathetic and compassionate toward them.

- *Look for similarities.* Because of confirmation bias, you will be more likely to feel empathy and compassion for someone who is 'just like you'. Consciously focus on similarities between you and the person you are listening to, not differences. For instance: You both have families, you both live in the same town, you both want to feel happy and successful ... the similarities are endless! Ask yourself, "How is this person just like me?"
- *Consider the other person first.* When you are feeling like your heart is closed, ask yourself, "Am I focused on 'me first' and what negative things might happen to *me* if I open my heart? Of am I focused on how I could help the other person?" If you find that you are focusing on yourself and possible negative ends that could happen, ask yourself: "What am I afraid of, and why?" Seeing that fear and then dispelling it will help you open your heart.

If you don't know how to open your heart, please don't despair. Just practice. Practice the Think Kindly, Speak Kindly and Act Kindly behaviors. Practice *checking in with people*, and not on them and listening deeply. Do the best that you can. Then be kind to yourself and practice some more. Through that practice you will learn to open your heart. And you will model that learning for others and lead by kind example. That is what this book, and kind leadership is all about.

KLC Stop & Think Point Noticing that your heart isn't open is a clue that as a Leader, you are putting yourself and your needs ahead of your people. Put on your Leader Hat and think about how you can overcome your fears and open your heart to consider others first, even if you don't agree with them.

Listening with open eyes, open ears, open mind and an open heart takes a lot of conscious practice. It's something that everyone can work to improve. To help you practice each of the four areas, go to this chapter's Practice Section and complete the exercises (Figure 6.5 and Figure 6.6) on pages 132. (You can stop and do the exercises now or continue reading and do them at the end of this chapter.)

Act Kindly Behavior 3: Recognize Others

The third key Act Kindly behavior is *Recognize others,* and it flows out of the first two Act Kindly behaviors. That's because in order to truly recognize others, you need to see them as 'people' and listen to them with open eyes, open ears, open mind and an open heart. For Kind Leaders, *recognizing others* has two parts. The first is recognizing people's efforts on a daily basis and the second is truly recognizing them for being the 'people' that they are.

Recognize the Means Instead of the Ends

If you've ever worked for a large organization, I'm going to bet that it probably had some sort of formal program in which employees were 'recognized'. Perhaps employees received a monetary bonus for completing a large project, a trophy of some sort for being in the top ten producers, or maybe, if their performance was really outstanding, they were invited on a special trip or to some kind of awards ceremony for high achievers. I've worked in many such organizations. And although I actually won those awards, and it might have made me feel good about some of my accomplishments, in the end, it didn't make me feel 'recognized' for who I was as a person.

Take a moment, put your Follower Hat on and think back to a time you worked in an organization with that type of 'recognition' program. (And if you haven't worked in this type of organization, that's okay. Think back to a sports program you were in, or back to when you were in school. Most sports programs and schools have formal recognition programs too.) Were most people satisfied with the recognition program as a whole? Did people believe that those who were recognized deserved the recognition, or was there a lot of jealousy and talking about those people behind their backs? Did the same people tend to be recognized over and over? If you weren't one of those people, how did you feel? About yourself, about the people who won, and about the organization in general? Now, keeping your Follower Hat on, think about the answer to this last question: Were the people who won the awards recognized for the effort they put in (the means) regardless of the outcome, or were the end results the 'thing' that what was recognized?

In many organizations, formal recognition programs focus solely on the 'ends'. Recognition is saved for a job or project completed and deemed to be 'well done'. In general, the recognition is focused not on the person who did the work, but on the work itself. A thing: 'The new client onboarding automation project that Sally Jones worked on'. As you've seen throughout this book, kind leadership doesn't focus on the 'ends' or 'things'. For Kind Leaders, *recognizing others* isn't about formal programs and about *what* employees did for the organization, it's about the means: leaders recognizing the time and effort their people contribute on a daily basis and thanking them for it. Yes, actually saying the words 'thank you' each and every day.

You may be thinking to yourself, "How am I going to thank people for the work they do every single day. I don't even know what most of my employees do". The answer goes right back to the first key Act Kindly behavior. When you spend time *checking in* with your people, as well as getting to know them as 'people', you'll see the effort they are putting into their work on a daily basis. As Jim Semple walked the floor of his plant each day, *checking in*, he noticed something: "People are starving for acknowledgment, recognition and praise. Give it to them, genuinely and sincerely, and you'll have their loyalty for life. There is no downside and no cost".[15] Thanking people on a daily basis recognizes the effort they put in day after day, which, for Kind Leaders, is much more important than the end results.[16]

Like all the other Kind Leader key behaviors, creating a daily 'recognition practice', takes practice. Here are some ideas to get you started:

- *Ask people to show you what they are working on.* During your daily *check ins* ask people to show you the work they are doing. Then *listen with open eyes and open ears* to the tone of their voice and watch their body language. What are the parts of their work that they are proud of? What did they learn to do that they didn't know yesterday? What tricky pieces of work are they diligently figuring out how to do? Those will give you clues about what to say thank you for today.
- *Be specific in your recognition.* Once you see and hear what the person is working on, thank them for a specific part of that work: "Jeff, thank you so much for explaining that to our customer so patiently. It would have been so easy to let your frustration show in your voice, but you didn't. Your patience really helped the whole situation", instead of just saying, "Thanks, Jeff, for your time and effort today". Focusing your thanks on the means makes people feel recognized and it models kind leadership behavior as well.

- *Say 'thank you' no matter what the results.* No one has a good day every day! When you hear sadness, frustration or disappointment in someone's voice and see it in their body language, *listen with an open mind and an open heart.* Then think about what you can thank the person for: "Linda, I know you had hoped to turn that client around and get them to stay on our service. Thank you for persevering. Your effort is really appreciated". Thanking people when things don't go right creates trusting relationships and a culture of trust as well because people know there's no reason for them to be afraid.

Although it may seem too easy to be true, it isn't. *Recognizing others* starts with *checking in* with them, *listening with open eyes, open ears, open mind and an open heart*, and then simply saying thank you for their time and effort. And sincerely meaning it. Because every day, your people make the choice to spend their precious time helping your organization instead of spending it elsewhere. When you say thank you both in words, and by spending your precious time with them, they will feel that their efforts are important and that their contributions are truly recognized.

Recognize People for Who They Are as People

Do you remember the story at the beginning of Chapter 2 that Debbie Eison told about her client? It's the story about when Debbie asked her client about their experience with leadership and kindness. What her client remembered was that the CEOs, Vice Presidents and Directors of companies she worked for had walked right by people in the hall without looking at them or speaking to them (unless the leaders needed something). And that those same leaders never acknowledged their people, the work they did, or said thank you. Years later, what Debbie's client remembered was the awful feeling of seeming invisible to leadership. What stuck in Debbie's client's mind – and heart – was the disappointment and hurt that comes from not being *recognized as a person*. That's why *recognizing people for who they are as 'people'* is the second part of this third key Act Kindly behavior.

As human beings, people don't just want to be recognized for the work that they do and the time and effort they put into their work. What people want is to be recognized for being the whole people that they are. As Jim Semple, whom you met above says, "Everybody questions themselves; their competence; their self-worth. The greatest act of kindness is showing people you believe in them, that you've got their back".[17] Leaders don't just need to recognize and be thankful for people's time, effort and work, they need to recognize the joys, challenges and struggles their people go through as people.

As a Kind Leader, the way to *recognize people for who they are as people,* is to listen carefully to what they need and then help them. Help them not with what you think they need, and in the ways you think they need it, but with what *they* need, and in the ways that *they* need it. As Amir Ghannad said in Chapter 2, "It's not 'do unto others as you would like to have done unto you', but 'do unto others as they would like to be done to them' ".[18] When Amir's wife and daughter were in a near fatal accident, Amir's leader helped Amir navigate through a very difficult part of his life. Stewart Bellamy invited his new quality assurance person to Christmas dinner so that he and his wife wouldn't be alone for the holidays in a new city. The leader of the team that I was on many years ago made sure that the person who was having mental health issues was supported and treated kindly by coworkers when they returned to work. No one is perfect. Every person has hopes and dreams, strengths and weakness and successes and challenges. Because everyone brings their whole self with them wherever they go (whether they're asked to leave part of themself at home or not!), *recognizing people as people* means accepting each person for who they are and then helping them become the person that *they* want to be. How do you, as a Kind Leader do that? Here are some suggestions:

- *Don't assume. Ask.* Each of the people who follow you is different. Things that might be helpful for one person, might not be helpful for another. Instead of assuming what a person wants, have a conversation with them and ask. Then you can listen with open eyes, open ears, open mind and an open heart and decide, with the person, what to try. And if two of your people seem to be having the same problem, don't assume that what will help one will help the other. Ask!
- *If something seems off, ask.* When you check in with people every day, and get to know them as people, you will be able to tell when something seems 'off'. Maybe the person is usually smiling and cheerful, and they seem strangely quiet or subdued. Or maybe they are usually quiet but appear quite agitated. If the person isn't acting like they usually do, spend some time asking them what's going on, and how they think you could help.
- *Reassure people that no one is perfect, and that they don't need to be.* Tell people about the mistakes you make and the problems that you have. Share your life with them as well. Remind people that they aren't

'valued' for what they do and the 'results' of their work, but that they are cared for and accepted for who they are as whole people.

As a Kind Leader, *recognizing people for who they are as people* means interacting with them, caring for them and helping them like you would a friend or family member. Walking down the street, when you see someone you *recognize*, you smile, say hello and stop and chat. As a leader, when you walk down the halls of your organization, that's how it should be as well. Smile, say hello, and recognize your people. And if you don't know someone, take a few moments, ask them their name, introduce yourself and find out who they are, as a person. Not just what their role is in your organization. To help you practice *recognizing others*, go to this chapter's Practice Section and complete the exercise (Figure 6.7). (You can stop and do the exercises now or continue reading and do it at the end of this chapter.)

Leading by Kind Example Creates a World of Kindness

Actively practicing the key Think, Speak and Act Kindly behaviors and *leading by kind example* is how Kind Leaders create trust and spread kindness throughout their organization and beyond. You might not be surprised to find out that Jim Semple, who *checked in* frequently with his people, was Stewart Bellamy's leader. Stewart, who followed Jim's kind leadership example and invited his new quality assurance person to celebrate the holidays with him was in turn invited to celebrate with the quality assurance person's family. When Amir Ghannad, who had been treated kindly by his manager, became the manager of his own plant, he created the Cradle of Prosperity initiative to help those he was leading in ways they needed to be helped. The wonderful thing about leading by kind example is that it doesn't just stay within the organization, it spreads to other places when followers put on their Leader Hats in other areas of their lives and imitate the kind behaviors their leaders have modeled.

When I asked my own mentor, Leslie Henckler, to tell me a story about a time a leader was kind to her, she told me about how, when she was struggling to teach others a new way to work, she reached out to a leader much higher in the organization, who she didn't know, to ask for help. That leader immediately came to Leslie's aide, helped her without asking anything in return, and in time, became Leslie's mentor and very good friend.[19] As Leslie was telling me this story, I broke in and said:

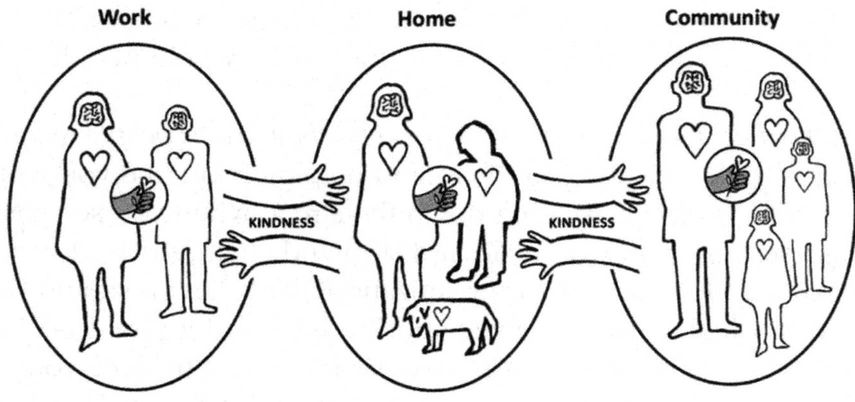

Figure 6.2 Kindness spreads through leading by kind example.

> Leslie, I know this is supposed to be the story about how a leader was kind to *you*, but it's also the story about how, as a leader, you were kind to *me*. Because what you are describing is exactly how I met you.

More than ten years ago, while working as an entry-level customer service representative and trying to create better ways to help my customers, I reached out to Leslie, a senior leader working far away in the company's corporate office. Although Leslie didn't know me, she immediately offered to help, flying half-way across the country to show me what to do. And Leslie's help didn't stop there. She supported me on a daily basis even though she was never my direct manager. Just like Leslie's leader became one of Leslie's closest friends, Leslie became one of my best friends as well. When a leader leads by kind example, that's how followers will lead when they put on their Leader Hat.

One Last Thought…

Before ending this chapter and the book's section on The Three Key Kind Leader Practices, I'd like to leave you with one last thing to think about. Although people often believe that changing their thinking is the key to changing their behavior, I believe it's the other way around. That changing how you act, what you do – *your practice* – is what changes your thoughts. The way you act changes how you think. And that's why it's so important to practice. The more often you practice the Speak Kindly behaviors of *Choose your words kindly*, *Use a kind tone of* voice and *If it's not kind, don't say it*, and the Act Kindly behaviors of *Checking in with people, not on them*, *Listening*, and *Recognizing others*, the easier it will become for you to Think Kindly. And the easier it is for you to Think Kindly, the more often you will Speak and Act Kindly too. It is all interconnected and works together.

Now, as I'm sure you've guessed, since this Discussion is done, it's time to practice!

Practice: Practical Exercises to Use to Turn Your Thoughts into Action

How often do you check in with your people? How much time do you spend with them each day? How well do you know them and how much do you know about them as whole people? How often do you thank them? The three key Acting Kindly Behaviors: *Checking in with People, Listening with Open Eyes, Open Ears, Open Mind and an Open Heart, and Recognizing Others* are practices that take deliberate, conscious and constant effort. You may not practice them at all now, you may spend some time practicing them, or you may spend quite a bit of time practicing them already. Wherever you are in your practice, these exercises are designed to help you move forward. Through practice there is always a way to act more kindly and improve your ability to lead by kind example. And because you can always improve, I suggest you make copies of these exercises and practice as often as you can.

Exercise 1: How Well Do You Know Your People as People?

As a leader, you need to get to know your people as 'people'. That means knowing who they are beyond their job or role description in your organization. List the names of five of your people, and without asking them, fill in the information in each column. If you don't know the answer, leave it blank. When you're finished, look and see how much you know and how much you don't. Are you surprised? How can you find out more and 'fill in the blanks'?

How well do you know your people as people? Checking in with people means getting to know them as whole people. Put on your Leader Hat and take some time to see how much you know about your people. Then use this chart to spend time getting to know people and 'filling in the blanks'!				
Person's Name	What are their family members' names?	What are they most passionate about?	What are they most concerned about?	What don't you know about them?

Figure 6.3 Checking in with people means getting to know them as people!

Exercise 2: How Are You Spending Your Precious Time?

There are lots of demands on your time as a leader. It's easy for a whole day to go by and not be sure where the time went and how you spent it. If you're not conscious of how you're spending your time, you might find you're spending too much of it on 'things' and not enough of it with people. Fill out this chart over a week. What do you see? If you aren't spending enough time with your people, what will you do?

How are you spending your precious time?

To become conscious of how you are spending your time currently, put on your Leader Hat and fill out this chart and 'see'.

Each day, list the number of minutes and hours you're spending on different activities.

Are you spending your time on 'things' or are you spending your time with your people?

Day and Date	Checking in with my people	In meetings with others	Checking email and reading reports	Other Activities (List each activity)
Monday:				
Tuesday:				
Wednesday:				
Thursday:				
Friday:				
Total:				

Figure 6.4 How much of your time are you spending with your people?

Exercise 3: Listening with Open Eyes and Open Ears

This exercise is designed to help you focus on listening with *open eyes* and *open ears*. For each conversation you have with someone, make a special effort to pay attention to the person's body language, surroundings and tone of voice and word choices. Record what you see and hear in this chart. Then reflect on what you could do to improve next time. And it's okay to tell the person you are listening to that you are practicing. It will model kind behavior for them too!

Listening with open eyes and open ears Wearing your Leader Hat, practice listening with open eyes and open ears by making notes after each conversation you have. What was the person's body language? What did you see in their surroundings? What words were used and what were their meanings? What tones of voice did you hear? What did you learn about your listening? How could you listen better next time?		
Topic/Person	**What do I see?**	**What do I hear?**
Conversation #1 **How could I listen better?**	**Body Language:** **Surroundings:**	**Denotative words:** **Connotations:** **Tone:**
Conversation #2 **How could I listen better?**	**Body Language:** **Surroundings:**	**Denotative words:** **Connotations:** **Tone:**
Conversation #3 **How could I listen better?**	**Body Language:** **Surroundings:**	**Denotative words:** **Connotations:** **Tone:**
Conversation #4 **How could I listen better?**	**Body Language:** **Surroundings:**	**Denotative words:** **Connotations:** **Tone:**

Figure 6.5 Better listening starts with practicing 'seeing' and 'hearing' others.

Exercise 4: Listening with Open Mind and an Open Heart

Similar to the previous exercise, this one is designed to help you focus on listening with *open mind* and an *open heart*. For each conversation you have, note whether you are closed- or open-minded and hearted. Then reflect on why you thought and felt the way you did. What could you do to both open your mind and heart and improve your listening next time?

Listening with an open mind and open heart Wearing your Leader Hat practice listening with an open mind and open heart. Pay special attention to when you are closed-minded and closed-hearted. What made you think and feel that way? How could you overcome it? What did you learn about your listening? How could you listen better next time?		
Topic/Person	**What do I see?**	**What do I hear?**
Conversation #1 **How could I listen better?**	**Was I closed or open minded?:** **What did the person say, and how did they say it that made me think that way?:**	**Was I closed or open hearted?:** **What did the person say, and how did they say it that made me think that way?:**
Conversation #2 **How could I listen better?**	**Was I closed or open minded?:** **What did the person say, and how did they say it that made me think that way?:**	**Was I closed or open hearted?:** **What did the person say, and how did they say it that made me think that way?:**
Conversation #3 **How could I listen better?**	**Was I closed or open minded?:** **What did the person say, and how did they say it that made me think that way?:**	**Was I closed or open hearted?:** **What did the person say, and how did they say it that made me think that way?:**
Conversation #4 **How could I listen better?**	**Was I closed or open minded?:** **What did the person say, and how did they say it that made me think that way?:**	**Was I closed or open hearted?:** **What did the person say, and how did they say it that made me think that way?:**

Figure 6.6 Better listening ends with practicing being open-minded and open-hearted.

Exercise 5: Recognizing Your People Means Saying Thank You for Their Effort

Are you walking down the halls with your eyes on your device, or are you 'recognizing' each person you pass? Use this chart to note how many people you 'recognize' each day. Are you thanking them for their time and effort, or only the result? How are helping people according to what their needs?

Thank you … and how can I help? Who did you thank today? Who did you help today? To create a strong recognition practice, write down each person you thanked or helped each day. If you had difficulty thinking about how to say thank you or help someone, take time to reflect on why. Then practice some more!	
Person and Situation	**How I thanked them for their effort or helped them**

Figure 6.7 Recognizing others means thanking them for their effort and helping as needed.

Reflection: What Would You Do? Kind Leader Practice Scenarios

Now that you've had the opportunity to read the ideas and theory presented in the Discussion section and do the Practice exercises, it's time to reflect on what you've learned and proactively plan how to apply those learnings.

In the last chapter, both Kay'La Janson and Kevin Landrell were dealing with difficult situations. I wonder what happened and how they are doing now? Let's check in with them and see.

Leading by Kind Example Leads to Leading by Kind Example

Scenario – Kay'La and Kevin's Stories: There's Always a Way to Lead by Kind Example...

Kay'La Janson sat down at her desk, booted up her laptop and clicked on the link to start the video chat. In just a few moments, Kevin Landrell's face popped into the window on the screen. As Kay'La waited for Kevin's audio to connect, she thought to herself, "When I was growing up, being able to talk to someone by video chat was just science fiction! I had to stand in line with my siblings to get my one minute per week to talk to my grandparents because 'long distance' was so expensive on the telephone! It's really quite amazing to be able to see people even when we can't be with them in person. I can check in with people all around the 'Codstom world' and get a good sense of what's happening by what I see and hear and then I can figure out how to help them". Since receiving the email from Cindy Yang that Kevin had forwarded to her, Kay'La had been checking in with Kevin on a weekly basis. As a new supervisor, Kay'La knew that Kevin needed all the help he could get. She could remember what it was like when she got her first management role and how much the help she received Darnell Laker, her branch manager, had meant to her. No matter how busy he was, Darnell always had time to chat through tricky situations with Kay'La. In fact, once he'd even stepped out of a meeting he was having with the company's Vice Presidents to take her call. Even now, years later, if Kay'La was really stuck, she knew she could call Darnell and he'd be there to listen and help. "I'm so happy I can help Kevin in the same way", Kay'La thought to herself.

As Kevin's audio finally connected, Kay'La turned her full attention to listening to what he had to say. "Things are definitely better here than they were last week. It's been a lot of listening and a lot of work, but we seem to be getting somewhere. The meeting we had with you, Cindy, Molly and I was tense at first, but hearing which words are acceptable to use, and which aren't, right from you, seems to have made a big impression, at least on Molly. Molly took the list you sent and printed it out and hung it up in her cubicle. And your idea to have Molly do a team training about what words we can and can't use with clients and each other was brilliant. Since she gave the training, Molly has been watching her own words, and listening to what others are saying and how they are saying it". Kay'La smiled to herself. It was wonderful to hear what Kevin was saying, and the smile he had on his face lit up the screen. "How is Cindy doing?" Kay'La asked. Before Kevin could answer, she could see his brow furl and his shoulders slump. "Well, I'm not sure. She's pretty much closeted herself in her office with the door closed. And every time I knock on the door, she just waves me away. I've been trying to connect with her, but I think she's still pretty mad about the whole thing. And there's been some rumors going around the office that she's been having some kind of family problems too. Some people have been saying it's probably her own fault because she never speaks nicely to anyone, but you just never know. Maybe she's in a bad temper when she's here because of whatever is going on at home". Kevin's voice trailed off and he looked down at his keyboard.

"Don't worry, Kevin", Kay'La said reassuringly. "Thank you for trying to reach out to her. And for your effort to help people see that situations usually aren't as clear as they seem. People have complicated lives, and it's our job as leaders to help them as much as we can. It doesn't always happen immediately though. So, don't be discouraged. I have a few other ideas that we can try. This week, why don't we …".

Now It's Your Turn to Reflect and Apply

Put on your Leader Hat and think about what you would do in this situation. If you were Kay'La, what would you suggest to Kevin? How would you help him learn and grow as a Kind Leader? What about Cindy? How could you help her? If you were Kevin, how could you continue to help Molly and your team, and not be discouraged about your lack of progress helping Cindy? What could you do to lead by kind example for the rest of the branch? Write your ideas here:

Chapter 6 Kind-Points

- *The Three Key Act Kindly Behaviors are Check in With People, Not on Them, Listen: With Open Eyes, Open Ears, Open Mind and an Open Heart and Recognize Others.* The three key behaviors are interconnected and flow from each other. Acting Kindly links back to Thinking Kindly, because actions influence thoughts. So, the more kindly you act, the more kindly you will think.
- *Check in with People, Not on Them. Checking in with people* means getting to know and care about the people who work for you as whole *people*. To do that you need to spend time with them, where they are, to see how they are feeling, how they are doing, and what help they need. People are never 'things' to be 'checked on'.
- *Listen: With Open Eyes, Open Ears, Open Mind and an Open Heart.* For Kind Leaders, listening is an active behavior that helps them focus on the 'means' and hear what their people need. Listening isn't easy for anyone, and it can be particularly hard for leaders, so leaders need to spend a lot of time practicing listening.
- *Recognize Others.* Recognizing others has two parts. First, it means recognizing the time and effort people contribute and thanking them for it, regardless of the end result. Second, it means accepting and caring about each person for the unique individual that they are. When you walk down the hallways of your organization, you should recognize and connect with every person as you would your friends and family.
- *Leading by Kind Example Creates a Kinder World.* From the Kind Leader point of view, leading by kind example means *deliberately acting and reacting with kindness to generate positive effects and outcomes for others.* When leaders lead by kind example, followers imitate those behaviors when they have their Leader Hats on. This is the way that kindness spreads within organizations and throughout the world.

Notes

1. www.merriam-webster.com/dictionary/example Downloaded April 1, 2021.
2. Personal interview with Jim Semple, August 10, 2020.
3. Personal interview with Amir Ghannad, October 19, 2020.
4. Personal interview with Stewart Bellamy, October 7, 2020.
5. Personal interview with Cheryl Jensen, November 9, 2020.
6. Optimal Hours with 'The Boss' Study, https://cdn.shopify.com/s/files/1/0860/7364/files/Leadership_IQ_Whitepaper_Optimal_Hours_with_the_Boss_Study_2014.pdf?4279660079233060856 Downloaded January 5, 2021.
7. Personal interview with Jim Semple, October 8, 2020.
8. Personal interview with Stewart Bellamy, October 7, 2020.
9. Optimal Hours with 'The Boss' Study, https://cdn.shopify.com/s/files/1/0860/7364/files/Leadership_IQ_Whitepaper_Optimal_Hours_with_the_Boss_Study_2014.pdf?4279660079233060856 Downloaded January 5, 2021.
10. Dick Lee and Delmar Hatesohl, Listening: Our Most Used Communications Skill, https://extension.missouri.edu/cm150 Downloaded January 9, 2020.
11. Ibid.
12. Stacey Hanke, This Important Leadership Skill isn't Hard to Master, but Most Don't Do It. www.entrepreneur.com/article/305977 Downloaded January 9, 2020.
13. Iqra Noor, Confirmation Bias, www.simplypsychology.org/confirmation-bias.html Downloaded January 11, 2021.
14. We Only Hear What We Want to Hear, https://exploringyourmind.com/only-hear-want-hear/ Downloaded January 11, 2021.
15. Personal interview with Jim Semple, August 10, 2020.
16. Please remember these practices work in every leadership situation. Recognizing people by thanking them for their time and effort is as important at home and out in the community as it is at work.
17. Personal interview with Jim Semple on October 8, 2020.
18. In person interview with Amir Ghannad, October 20, 2020.
19. Personal interview with Leslie Henckler on November 25, 2020.

Chapter 7

Collaboration, Cooperation and Kindness, Not Competition

A kind leader can make a world of difference.

Linda Michelle Cohen

Discussion – Beyond Win–Win: A World of Kindness

One of the best things about kind leadership is that when leaders act, react and lead by kind example, the outcome is more kindness as their followers imitate those kind behaviors in the situations where they wear their Leader Hats. Whether kind leadership starts at work, at home or somewhere else in the community, it doesn't just stay there, it spreads. And all of the positive benefits spread as well: a focus on the 'means', instead of the 'ends', the creation of trusting personal relationships and wider circles of trust, and the practice of considering others first. As kindness spreads, there are broader benefits for organizations and society, including moving from fear-based competitive ways of interacting towards kinder ones like collaboration, cooperation, and those that move 'beyond win-win' to true kindness.

DOI: 10.4324/9781003141433-7

The Kind Leadership Continuum

Over time, as they spread, kind leadership practices also lead to better ways for people and groups to *interact together* within organizations, in communities, in wider society and across the world. Please take a very close look at Figure 7.1. It's an illustration of what I call The Kind Leadership Continuum and it shows what happens to people's *interactions* as leaders become kinder. On the far left-hand side of the Continuum, where leaders don't consciously practice kind leadership (or are outright deliberately unkind), interactions between people are fearful, distrustful and divisive. As leaders develop their ability to Think, Speak and Act Kindly they will be able to influence their followers' interactions to move along the Continuum to the right towards harmony, trust and unity. Since followers wear Leader Hats in other situations and places, they, in turn, will influence those they lead to make progress along the Continuum as well.

It's also important for you to pay close attention to where your people's interactions are on the Continuum so that you can gain insight into where *you* need to deepen your Kind Leader practice. If your followers' interactions aren't advancing toward the right, or if they are retreating towards the left, then you know that your behavior, as a leader, needs to change. Because interactions between individuals and groups impact how we all live together in society and the world, it's critical that you know where your followers are on the Continuum and what behavior you need to change to influence them to be kinder.

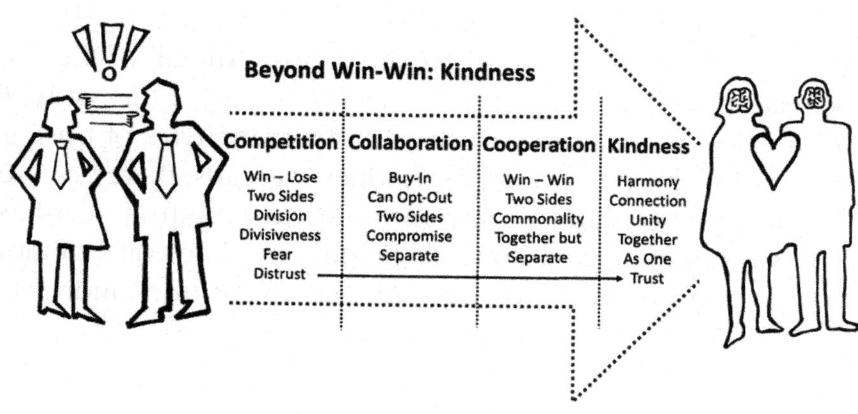

Figure 7.1 The Kind Leadership Continuum.

As a Kind Leader, to help your people move along the Continuum, you'll have to pay careful attention to how they are interacting right now and understand where those interactions fall on The Kind Leadership Continuum. What is the best way to do that? Spend time checking in with them and listening, with open eyes, open ears, open mind and an open heart. When you walk through the halls, what do you see? Are people smiling and saying hello to each other? If not, why aren't they interacting? When you check in, are people complimenting others or complaining about the lack of help their coworkers are giving them? If they are complaining about others, what does it tell you about their interactions? How are people interacting in meetings? Are some people obviously stopped from talking by a glare or the raised eyebrows of others? As a leader, every time you are with a group of people, there is an opportunity to pay close attention to their interactions and to look for clues as to where they are on The Kind Leadership Continuum. Once you see where they are, then you can decide both what to do to help them move towards kinder ways of interacting, and what you need to work on in your own Kind Leader practice.

As you pay attention to how people *interact*, you're going to notice that throughout your organization and even within one area or team, there's a wide variety of interaction types. Some may be competitive, some collaborative, some cooperative and some kind. That's normal and to be expected. Simply work with each area and each person and help them shift toward the right on the Continuum. Throughout the rest of this chapter, you'll learn about each of the different types of interactions (competition, collaboration, cooperation and kindness), what to look for to recognize where your people are on the Continuum, and what you need to do to improve your kind leadership practice to help them progress.

Competition: Win–Lose Interactions

Two-sides – Division – Divisiveness – Fear – Distrust

On the left hand-side of The Kind Leadership Continuum, you'll see the first, and least kind type of interaction: *Competition*. Although many traditional leadership models are based on competition and some think that 'competition brings out the best in people', unfortunately, in terms of kindness, competition brings out the worst in people. According to the

Merriam-Webster dictionary, competition is defined as, "to strive consciously or unconsciously for an objective (such as position, profit, or a prize); be in a state of rivalry. (Synonyms: battle, contend, face-off, fight, rival, and vie)".[1] Whether at work, at home, or in politics, competitive interactions create divisiveness and fear because in a competition, there are only two possibilities: winning and losing, and whoever wins gains power over whoever loses. In competitive interactions people 'assume negative intent' about each other which results in them speaking and acting unkindly. This causes three effects that as you've seen throughout this book aren't compatible with kindness: fear, 'ends'-orientation and a focus on self instead of others.

Because competitive interactions are often looked upon favorably in many traditional leadership models (a little 'healthy competition never hurt anyone'), and because many people spend a lot of their time in competitive environments (results-oriented workplaces) and pursuits (playing and watching sports), as a leader, you're going to have to look consciously and carefully to see where competitive interactions are causing negative unkind effects in your organization. Look especially for those that are associated with fear. Competition and fear go hand in and hand and fear both causes, and is a result of, competition. When people are afraid of losing (their paycheck, their job, a desired promotion), they are likely to become even more competitive. And the more competitive people become, the greater the fear of losing becomes, the more likely it is that they will act and react in unkind ways. For example: Even if your work was recognized and you won the bonus competition last quarter, unless you work harder and are more competitive, you might not win it next quarter, so why bother spending time helping your co-worker's project succeed? When it comes to fear and competition, not only do you 'reap what you sow', you 'sow what you reap'.

KLC Stop & Think Point: What do you think about competition? How much time do you spend in competitive interactions? Put on your Leader Hat and think about whether those interactions focus you on the 'ends' and how you can win, or if they focus you on others, which is where Kind Leaders need to focus?

Here's What to Look for

To see if your people and organization are in the competitive interaction part of The Kind Leadership Continuum, here's what you need to look for:

- *Fearful behaviors.* When people are afraid, they behave in one of three ways: fight, flight, or freeze. Although 'fight' is the easiest behavior to see, flight and freeze are also signs of fear and competition.
  - *Fight*: Pay careful attention to how your people get along with each other in many situations. First, although it may not happen often, make sure that you are notified of any physical altercations that occur in your organization. Next, look for incidents of people arguing with each other both verbally and in writing in email and text messages. When people are together, do you see them 'fighting' strenuously to get their point across or badgering others into conceding? All of these are signs of the 'fight' response to fear that comes from competition.
  - *Flight*: Is there a lot of turnover or absenteeism in your area or organization? Has there been an increase? Turnover and absenteeism are both good indicators that people might be 'fleeing' because they are afraid. Other indicators are people who don't show up to meetings, or find reasons to be away from their work-space during the times that you are planning to check-in with them. Be vigilant, because 'Flight' responses are a way that people can try to hide their fear from you.
  - *Freeze*: Think about a 'deer caught in the headlights'. When you ask a person a question, and they have that kind of look on their face, or if they are unable to move forward with their work, they could be 'frozen' with the fear of making a mistake or failing.
- *Creating paper-trails and over-documenting*: Another type of fearful behavior that's a result of competition is over-documentation and creating paper-trails. This occurs when people are afraid that they are going to be blamed for errors. If you are copied on scores of long email strings, ask yourself what is causing people to be so afraid that they need to document every conversation and interaction.
- *Lack of empathy and compassion.* When you are checking in with people, listen to the way that they talk about their co-workers and customers. Do they have empathy and compassion for the situations

others are in? Or are they focused on themselves, and their needs only? Do they complain about the problems others cause them, and then brag about their own accomplishments? Lack of empathy, compassion and caring for others and a focus on self and bragging about accomplishments are evidence of competition.
- *Ends and numbers focus.* I once worked in an organization in which job grade was the first thing people discussed when getting to know each other! Needless to say, this was an organization that had an extremely competitive culture. As you saw in Chapter 3, when there is a focus on 'numbers' and 'making those numbers', fear is sure to follow. As a leader, look for interactions in which people are talking about the end-results and numbers only, without asking questions and focusing on 'how they got there'.
- *Performance management systems that rank and compare people.* Do you have a performance management system that compares people and marks them on various scales in relation to others? Are people's raises and bonuses then based on their ranking? Do managers and supervisors compare people's performance publicly during meetings? Look carefully at all the people management systems in your organization, because if they are 'ends-focused' and compare people, your organization is probably in the competitive interaction section of the Continuum.

Because competition is so common, and because fear creates a vicious cycle that spreads, it is likely that you will see many examples of competitive interactions and their unkind outputs and outcomes. That's why it's also so important for you, as a Kind Leader, to both look at the situation, and at yourself, and take action to move people away from competition and towards the kinder ways of interacting towards the right on the Continuum. Remember, kind leadership isn't just about theory and thinking, it's about action and doing. In the next section, you'll find out what to do to help people move 'to the right'.

Here's What to Do

If you find a preponderance of competitive interactions, here's what to do to move people away from competition and towards kinder ways of interacting:

- *Look at yourself first.* Are you thinking, speaking and acting in ways that are causing competition and fear in those you lead? If you are, then you need to spend time deeply reflecting on how you need to change your thoughts, words and actions so that instead of focusing on yourself, and the 'ends' first, your time is spent focusing on others and the 'means'.
  - *Think Kindly.* If you are assuming negative intent, spend time checking your thoughts about what and who you are 'competing' with that is causing you to be afraid. Perhaps you are applying for a promotion and are worried that one of your team member's negative performance numbers will prevent you from getting it. If that's the case, consciously change your unkind thoughts to kind ones instead.
  - *Speak Kindly.* Check your words. Are your thoughts and speech filled with competitive language? Like 'we need to win at all costs', or 'this project is high-stakes and failure is not an option'? If so, then change your words to kinder, less competitive ones, like 'It's not winning that counts, but how we play the game', and 'as long as we put in the effort, everything will be alright'.
  - *Act Kindly.* Make sure you are checking in with people, listening to them and recognizing their efforts. Maybe you have started checking on their results instead? Or maybe, you haven't been spending the time you need to with them at all. If that is the case, slow down, take time to reflect, and start checking in with people again.
- *Check in more frequently.* In order to understand why your people are afraid, you will need to spend more time 'checking-in' with each one individually and looking and listening for the underlying competitive interactions that are causing them fear. Are people having financial or other difficulties at home that are causing them to be fearful and compete with others for bonuses or promotions? If that is the case, figure out how to help them solve those problems. Are people being publicly 'punished' for making mistakes and 'rewarded' for succeeding? If so, put an end those practices and help managers learn how to focus on the means instead of the ends.
- *Reduce organizational practices that encourage competition.* If your organization has practices that compare people to each other and recognize and reward the 'ends' like annual performance reviews that rank and compare people in 'nine block performance grids' or along sprectrums from 'worst to best' performers, work to change

these policies to ones that aren't so competitive and pit person against person. (And team against team, because team rewards also create competition, just like they do in sports. You want people to trust and work with everyone in your organization, not just their teammates.) Focus on ways to thank and recognize people that you learned about in Chapter 6. Set up regular pay and work progression systems so that people don't have to be afraid that their effort won't be rewarded.
If this seems impossible, it isn't! When I teach classes in an online university program, as long as students turn in their work on time, they all receive an A in the course. I don't compare their work with others, and only look at the effort they put into learning. Once they are freed from the fear that comes with 'competing' for their grade, they can spend all their energy and time focused on getting the most out of the course and their learning.[2] Please remember, focusing on 'ends' and numbers instead of 'means' and effort guarantees competition and fear.
- *Create ways for people to work collaboratively and cooperatively.* As a Kind Leader, when you see people who are competing, and ways that they are working that cause competition, actively change those to collaborative and cooperative ones. 'Buddy' people up to help each other in areas where individual work now exists. Create cross-functional working groups and teams that force people to work together. Will this be messy and uncomfortable at first? Of course! You'll have to check in often and listen and recognize people's effort to work in new ways. With your support and care, they will get used to working with, instead of competing against, each other. And there's one more thing: Don't forget to model this behavior yourself. If you aren't collaborating and cooperating with others, and if your people don't see that you are working that way, they won't have your kind example to imitate.

Because competition is such an entrenched way of interacting with others, don't be discouraged if you find a lot of it in your organization, and in yourself. People are people, and have experiences in many places, so don't be surprised if someone who is interacting collaboratively, cooperatively or even kindly, reverts to interacting competitively. It's okay, and to be expected. Remember, no one, and no system is perfect. It's up to you, as a Kind Leader, to deepen your practice so that you can help others deepen theirs. That way, everyone can move toward kindness over time.

Before moving on to learn about collaborative interactions, put on your Leader Hat and think about your interactions and those of your people. How competitive are they? What do you see in yourself – and them – that tells you that, and what can you do to reduce the fear that results from, and causes, competition? To find out, go to this chapter's Practice Section and complete the exercise (Figure 7.2). (You can stop and do the exercise now or continue reading and do it at the end of this chapter.)

Collaboration: Interactions based on 'Buy-in'

Buy-in – Opt-Out – Two Sides – Compromise – Separate

Collaboration, the next type of interaction on The Kind Leadership Continuum is directly to the right of Competition and to the left of Cooperation. People often use collaboration and cooperation interchangeably, but, in terms of kind interactions, as you will see, they are different. That's why they are in separate categories on The Kind Leadership Continuum.

Collaboration, like competition, is a common style of interacting. In collaborative interactions, people may be organized to work in units, but the work they are doing is actually still separate. Think about call centers that are made up of hundreds of customer service representatives. Although organized into smaller teams each with their own supervisor, the service representatives all do basically the same job. Each customer service representative's 'performance' is measured individually, and there are also some team metrics and measures. Each team may be encouraged to create its own name and identity and share work internally to help 'lighten the load' of each team member. In this type of environment, people may share a 'collaborative' team goal, but in essence are still working individually. People are beginning to help each other, and focus outside of their own work and needs, but competitive interactions and behaviors can still be seen as people vie for position on the team.

Other examples of collaborative interactions are projects in which two or more areas of an organization work together for a short time to attain a specific goal, or a project in which a cross-functional team is put together to solve an internal problem. People are grouped together to achieve an end, but, again, are still primarily working separately.

The word collaborate is defined by the *Merriam Webster* dictionary as: "Work jointly with others or together" and has synonyms such as band together, concur, join, team-up, unite.[3] As you can see, this is a great first step towards kinder interactions, because instead of being outright rivals and vying to be the winner, people are working alongside others and beginning to work together.

For kind leadership, the most problematic element of working collaboratively is that that there are still separate and distinct sides. Think about a project team brought together to create an easier and more accurate way to keep track of up-sell requests from customers. The team is made up of salespeople, customer service representatives and IT people, each with their own 'agenda' from their area as well as individual wants, needs and goals. As the team works together, because they are still interacting from the perspective of their 'separate' points of view, a lot of time and energy is spent trying to get others on the team, and later in the organization, to 'buy-in' to their ideas and solutions. If it's not possible to get people to 'buy-in', then the team may arrive at a 'compromise'. That means that although neither 'side' gets exactly what they want, they 'broker a deal' in which most get some of what they want.

In collaborative interactions, because there are still two or more separate sides, one or more groups may feel that they have been 'coerced' into 'buying-in' because of an imbalance of power. And when people agree to a compromise because of that, they, themselves may feel unhappy, unheard, uncared for and 'compromised'. In fact, that's exactly how Pennie Saum felt in Chapter 4 when she was worried about working on a project with a department she had collaborated with in past. In collaborative interactions, there is less fear, and more trust, than in competition. But when fear comes back into the picture, people may decide to 'opt-out' of a compromise, and move back to the left of the Continuum to competition.

KLC Stop & Think Point: When you work collaboratively with others, do you put yourself and your own goals first, or do you consider others first? Put on your Leader Hat and think about how you can help the people who follow you consider others first when they are in collaborative interactions.

Here's What to Look for

To see if your people and organization are in the collaborative interaction part of The Kind Leadership Continuum, here's what you need to look for:

- *Separate but together.* People who are working collaboratively are still divided into two or more 'sides'. They are what I call 'separate but together'. Within your organization look for people who are grouped together on 'teams' but who really function as individuals. You can even see this in executive and other management level teams as leaders keep their silo's goals and needs in mind while working with others on organization wide initiatives.
- *Bargaining behaviors.* Bargaining behaviors in which one side tries to get the other side to 'buy in' are indicators of collaborative interactions. That's progress from competitive interactions in which the winning side doesn't take the losing side into account at all! When you see people are working on group projects or on shared work and you hear words and phrases about how one side can gain the other's 'buy-in', people are working collaboratively.
- *Compromises.* Collaboration can also involve a lot of compromises. Again, because two sides are still separate but striving toward 'working together', creating compromises between two or more ways is a good start. When you hear your people talk about how they came to a compromise to solve a problem, complete a project or reach a goal, then you are likely seeing collaborative interactions.

Here's What to Do

When you see collaborative interactions in your organization, here's what to do to recognize them and then encourage people to move even further to the right along The Kind Leadership Continuum towards cooperation.

- *Look at yourself first.* Are you thinking, speaking and acting in ways that encourage people to focus more on others first and less on themselves? That is best way to move beyond the idea of 'sides'.
  - *Think Kindly.* When you are working with others on your leadership team, or with the people who follow you, check your thoughts carefully to notice if you are automatically thinking of yourself, and

your 'side' first, or if you are thinking of others' wants, needs and perspectives first. If you find yourself thinking about yourself first, consciously work to change those thoughts.

- *Speak Kindly.* Listen carefully to the words you are choosing to use. Do you use a lot of bargaining words and phrases like 'I wonder how we can get people's buy-in', 'I have a counter-proposal' or 'Let's try to see if we can negotiate a compromise'? If you do, you are probably influencing others' language and behavior choices too.
- *Act Kindly.* Notice how you are acting during check ins. Are you recognizing collaboration and thanking people for their efforts? Are you listening carefully to hear why people are having a difficult time working together? Then are you helping them come up with better ways to collaborate and move towards interacting cooperatively?

- *Bring people together as 'people' more frequently.* One of the best ways to encourage people to think of others first and to continue collaborating and move towards cooperating is to have them get to know each other as 'people'. That way they can see the similarities in their lives, and focus less on the differences. Some ideas to bring people together as 'people' include spending time doing activities that involve people's family members and in which people don't talk about work. Time to volunteer to help others together (and inviting people's extended families to be included) is also a great way for people to come together and see each other as 'people' and friends. When people see similarities in each other, and view others as friends, they are more likely to think of their needs as well as their own.
- *Create more opportunities for people to work together.* How often do people get to work together in your organization? Really work together? Not just work in the same area on separate work, but really work together: to solve a problem or create a new service or product? If it's not often, create those opportunities for people to truly work together and pull them from diverse places in the organization. That's a great way for people get to know each other as 'people' as well!
- *Recognize collaborative efforts.* Whether you pull people together intentionally, or they organize themselves to work collaboratively, make sure to thank them and recognize their efforts, not just the results of their work. Otherwise instead of encouraging more collaboration people may revert to competitive interactions.

When you see collaborative interactions, celebrate! You are helping people move along The Kind Leadership Continuum, and when your followers wear their Leader Hats, they will be able to help others work more collaboratively and move further to the right of the Continuum, as well.

Cooperation: Interactions Based on 'Win–Win'

Win–Win – Two sides – Commonality – Together but Separate

Directly to the right of collaboration, and just before Kindness, you'll find *Cooperation*. Cooperative interactions differ from collaborative ones in a couple of significant ways. First, instead of 'win–lose' and bargaining, people strive toward 'win–win' solutions. That's because in cooperation, instead of focusing on differences and looking for compromises, people focus on commonality and solutions that are positive for both sides. Second, even though there are still 'sides' in cooperative interactions, as people move away from fear, toward trust, and see commonality, they work in ways that instead of being 'separate but together', are 'together but separate'.

The *Merriam-Webster dictionary* defines cooperation as: "To act or work with another or others; to associate with another or others for *mutual benefit*". Although the synonyms are the same as collaboration: band together, concur, join, team-up, unite,[4] as you can see there is a big difference in the definition. In cooperative interactions, people work together for mutual benefit, sometimes described as 'win–win'.

Cooperative 'win–win' interactions are less common than collaborative ones because cooperation involves putting others' needs first. To understand the difference between collaboration and cooperation, think about a cross-functional team pulled together to solve a difficult problem that affects the organization's customers and each of the team member's areas. In cooperation, team members band together to contribute as much as they can so that the customer benefits, instead of bargaining with each other to create compromises that protect their area. In this case, there are still two sides, but they aren't internal ones. The two sides are the organization, and the customer. By focusing outside of themselves, on their customer, the people working toward solving the problem come together to create a solution that is a 'win' for them, and a 'win' for the customer as well.

Cooperative ways of working involve considering others first and often come out of an increased ability to 'look for' and see commonality instead of differences. Cooperation comes from having empathy and compassion for others and blossoms as fear dissipates and trust grows. A number of years ago, I worked with Noah Goellner, the COO of Hennig Inc. Noah understood that the key to working more cooperatively organizationally was to focus on others, so he changed the company's mission statement to "Making Our Customers Successful!" Wherever work was being done in the company, the first question people asked themselves was "how will doing this make our customers successful"? Then they focused on figuring out the best ways to work together cooperatively so that each department could contribute solutions that would both make the customer successful and improve the work in the department. During COVID-19, as part of its cooperative way of working, Hennig Inc. made and provided hundreds of face shields to its local community hospital. As Noah said, "Now more than ever our community is our customer. So the question became: How can we make our community successful?" As Noah and Hennig Inc. found out, when people get together and truly cooperate, everyone 'wins'.[5]

Many larger problems, whether in organizations or across the world are complex, highly entrenched and seem intractable and unsolvable. Violence, war, poverty, discrimination and racial injustice stem from competition and vicious cycles of fear. Learning and practicing how to work together for the benefit of others, in cooperative interactions, is a step toward solving those problems and creating true kindness in the world for all.

As a Kind Leader, modeling cooperative interactions yourself, and encouraging those interactions between individuals and groups across the organization, will help create trust and give people the experience they need to model and teach others how to cooperate when they wear their Leader Hats.

KLC Stop & Think Point: How often do you truly work in a cooperative way with others? How do you actively model coming together to create 'win–win' solutions? Put on your Leader Hat and think about how you can actively model this yourself so that others can imitate ways of interacting cooperatively.

What to Look for

To see if your people are in the cooperative interaction part of The Kind Leadership Continuum, here's what to look for:

- *A focus on being of service to others.* Just like Hennig's mission of 'Making our customers successful', you know that you are seeing cooperative interactions when people are putting the needs of others before their own. They are working in 'service' of another person or group and their discussion and actions focus on how each can contribute so that everyone can be successful. Instead of hearing bargaining language and compromise, listen for phrases like "Here's how we could contribute" and "That will be a win for everyone".
- *'Together but separate'.* Cooperative interactions can be summarized by the phrase 'All for one and one for all'. Look for groups and teams that have metrics that focus on the collective 'means': how the entire team is making progress on working together in service of others and that aren't just measuring individual outcomes. The focus is on 'together' first.
- *Empathy and compassion.* Working cooperatively in service of others takes empathy and compassion. Look for people who are able to freely share their concerns about how others are feeling and what can be done to help them. Being able to recognize and freely share those feelings is a good sign of cooperative interactions.
- *Trust.* As interactions move from left to right on The Kind Leadership Continuum, trust increases. Hearing trusting language like "I'm not worried about getting behind because I know Sandy has my back and is always willing to help", and seeing trusting behaviors like easily sharing work and knowledge among team members are all excellent signs that people are interacting in cooperative ways.

Here's What to Do

When you see cooperative interactions in your organization, cherish and celebrate them!

- *Look at yourself first.* Celebrate your own successes in helping people move along The Kind Leadership Continuum towards true kindness! Then reflect and think about what else you can do to show people how to share feelings of empathy and compassion and come together in service of others.

- *Think Kindly.* Assuming the needs of others are positive and valid (assuming positive intent) encourages people to come together in service of others. Make your process of assuming positive intent visible so that others can imitate it.
- *Speak Kindly.* Use kind words and phrases that express empathy and compassion such as "I know how difficult it is for everyone to deal with the effects of the COVID-19 pandemic. Let's work together to see what we can do to make things better for all of us", and "I'm so appreciative of how you've all come together to support and care for Dale through the tough time his family is having" gives people phrases to imitate that support cooperative interactions.
- *Act Kindly.* When you check-in with people, recognize and thank them for their cooperation. Frequently. Recognizing people's effort to put others needs before their own and join together in service of something greater than themselves will let them know how appreciative you are of their efforts and how much you care.

- *Cooperative games and initiatives.* Use team building activities to create fun, cooperative ways for people to interact. In many organizations, teams compete against each other in challenges like mini-golf tournaments, chili cookoffs and costume contests. Instead of bringing people together cooperatively, these activities promote competition. To encourage cooperation, how about trying cooperative games in which the object is to solve a problem for mutual benefit?[6] Escape rooms and puzzles are great for this. Working with your local community on initiatives that would be beneficial for all is another great way to practice cooperative interactions.
- *Create common ground.* Invite your customers into your organization so that your people can get to know them as people. Then send your people out to spend time with your customers and their customers as well. When people spend time getting to know each other as 'people', they are more likely to look for (and see) how much they have in common, rather than what their differences are.
- *Recognize cooperative efforts.* Recognize, celebrate and thank people for their cooperative efforts. And not just your people, but all the

people involved. Customers, community members and everyone who cooperated to get to 'win–win'. The more people you bring together to recognize and celebrate, the better and kinder!

When you see cooperative interactions, celebrate! Not only are you helping people move along The Kind Leadership Continuum in your organization and helping your followers encourage cooperative interactions when they wear their Leader Hats, you're giving people practice in ways of interacting that can begin to solve the complex, difficult world problems created by the vicious cycle of fear that comes from competition.

Before starting the next section on Kindness, put on your Leader Hat and think about collaboration and cooperation in your organization. When people work together, how much collaboration do you see, and how much cooperation? Do people know what the difference is? How will you help them learn? Go to this chapter's Practice Section and complete the exercise (Figure 7.3). (You can stop and do the exercise now or continue reading and do it at the end of this chapter.)

Kindness: Interacting beyond 'Win–Win'

Harmony – Connection – Unity – Together – As One

In 2008, I took a course on conflict resolution that changed the way I did a lot of things and how I thought about them as well. As I learned about different types of conflict, from the most basic personal conflicts at level one, to the most complex intractable ones at level three,[7] something occurred to me: In all the strategies and ways that were described to resolve conflicts and bring people together, the idea of 'sides' always remained. You can see what I mean in the section above about cooperation. Even in cooperative interactions, where people work together and others' needs are considered with empathy and compassion, a solution that is 'win–win' still implies that there are two (or more) sides. Ultimately, what I realized, is that as long as there are 'sides' the potential for conflict and unkindness still exists. Because, even if one side 'buys-in' they can always decide to 'buy-out'. Solutions that were once viewed as 'win-win' could over time be seen differently, leaving the possibility of conflict, competition, fear and unkindness to arise again.

That is why I have added Kindness as the last type of interaction on The Kind Leadership Continuum. It is an aspirational one. A type of interaction in which 'sides' no longer exist. It is a type of 'oneness' in which people who work and live together don't see other people or groups as 'other' and 'separate' but as interconnected and one. The way I think about this kind of interaction is like an orchestra playing a beautiful symphony. Each instrument of each section plays a separate part, and the totality and beauty of the song that they create together is more than the sum of any one of those parts. What is created is harmony. Harmony not only for those playing, but for those listening, because those listening don't listen for and hear each part, only the totality of the creation. At the front of the orchestra stands the conductor. The person whose role it is to help each player become an interconnected part of the whole. The conductor is the person who imagines, and hears in their head, the beautiful possibility of what that harmony can be before it is created.

The Kind Leader is the conductor on The Kind Leadership Continuum. Both imagining a world of kindness and helping people move through the stages of the Continuum to get there. Imagining ways of being that move from separation and separateness toward connection and interconnection. From the vicious cycles of fear to the virtuous spread of kindness and peace. In the same way that the orchestra's conductor both imagines how beautiful the harmony will be when everyone plays together and then helps the symphony's musicians create that harmony, as a Kind Leader *you* need to both imagine and help your people interact in ever-kinder ways. Jean Paul Lederach describes this in his wonderful book, *The Moral Imagination*: "Stated simply, the moral imagination requires the capacity to imagine ourselves in a web of relationships that includes our enemies; the ability to sustain a paradoxical curiosity that embraces complexity without reliance on dualistic polarity; the fundamental belief in and pursuit of the creative act; and the acceptance of the inherent risk of stepping into the mystery of the unknown that lies beyond the far too familiar landscape of violence".[8]

In 2008, I wrote an essay for my class on beginning to imagine a world beyond 'win–win' interactions. The last paragraph of that essay says: "If we sow and reap violence and conflict, we will reap and sow violence; if we sow and reap cooperation and unity, we can transform seemingly intractable conflicts into fertile grounds for the seeds of harmony. Only we can break the cycle".[9] This book, and everything you find in it is a continuation of my work on both imagining and creating a world beyond 'win–win'. A world of Kindness on The Kind Leadership Continuum. I don't have the answers of what to look for and what to do to create this. I do know that as Kind Leaders, going forward, it's up to you and me to create them, through practice, together. Our world needs it.

To end this Discussion section and before going on to the Practice section, a quick reminder. The Kind Leadership Continuum is just that: a Continuum. So you, and the people you lead, can (and will) surge forward and slip backward. If you slip back don't worry, just keep practicing. Whether the last stage on the Continuum, Kindness is fully attainable or not doesn't matter. Working toward it will help you, as a leader, become kinder, the people who follow you to become kinder and that will create a kinder world. It's not a competition and there is never any failure in working on being kinder, so you don't have anything you need to fear!

Practice: Practical Exercises to Use to Turn Your Thoughts into Action

Helping your people interact more kindly and move along The Kind Leadership Continuum is just as important as helping them act, react and lead by kind example. As people interact more kindly at work, at home and in the community, when they are wearing both their Leader and Follower Hats, the world moves towards Kindness. In this section, you'll find two exercises designed to help you practice recognizing competitive, collaborative and cooperative interactions and help people move toward the right along The Kind Leadership Continuum. I've also added a 'visioning' exercise for you to complete to help you imagine what a world of Kind interactions would look like, and how you can help create it.

Exercise 1: How Competitive Is Your Organization? How Competitive Are You?

Competition and competitive interactions are a staple of many people's lives and many traditional leadership models. Unfortunately, competition, and the possibility of being the loser creates a lot of fear and that causes people to both act unkindly and become even more competitive. Look for competitive interactions in your organization and in your life. What cycles of fear do they create and what can you do to break those cycles?

How competitive is your organization? How competitive are you? With you Leader Hat on, actively look for competitive interactions and the fear that comes from them in your organization, and your personal interactions. Record what you see and feel. What can you do to break those cycles?		
Competitive Interaction	**Associated fear**	**Steps to reduce fear and competition**

Figure 7.2 Competitive interactions and the vicious cycle of fear go hand in hand.

Exercise 2: Collaboration? Cooperation? Do You Recognize Both?

When people in your organization work together, are they working collaboratively, cooperatively or both ways? How often do they collaborate and how often do they cooperate? Do you think they know the difference? What can you to do 'recognize' both types of interactions and move collaborative interactions towards cooperative ones?

Recognizing collaborative and cooperative interactions

When your people are working together look carefully to see when they are collaborating (bargaining behavior, language, 'win–lose' compromises) and when they are cooperating (putting other's first, 'win–win' and mutual benefit). How can you tell? How can you 'recognize' both and help move collaborative interactions towards cooperation?

Collaborative interactions	Cooperative interactions
What do I see? How can I recognize this effort? How can I help people move to cooperation?	What do I see? How can I recognize this effort?
What do I see? How can I recognize this effort? How can I help people move to cooperation?	What do I see? How can I recognize this effort? How can I help people move towards Kindness?
What do I see? How can I recognize this effort? How can I help people move to cooperation?	What do I see? How can I recognize this effort? How can I help people move towards Kindness?

Figure 7.3 Practice 'recognizing' collaboration and cooperation.

Exercise 3: Creating a World of Kind Interactions

In the space below, write and draw what Kindness, the interactions of the final stage on The Kind Leadership Continuum look like to you. Imagine a world of 'oneness' where all are interconnected and there is no fear, only trust. A world beyond 'win–win'. Thank you for helping me imagine it. And thank you for helping create it.

Reflection: What Would You Do? Kind Leader Practice Scenarios

Now that you've had the opportunity to read the ideas and theory presented in the Discussion section and do the Practice exercises, it's time to reflect on what you've learned and proactively plan how to apply those learnings.

In the last chapter, both Kay'La Janson and Kevin Landrell were dealing with difficult situations. I wonder what happened and how they are doing now? Let's check in with them and see.

Competition and Fear Don't go with Kindness

Scenario – Kay'La and Kevin's Stories: Together, as One, with Kindness, We Can Break the Vicious Cycle of Fear and Competition

Kevin Landrell was relieved that it almost time for his check-in with Kay'La Janson, Codstom's CEO. "I can't believe how much has happened in just one week", Kevin thought to himself. "If I didn't have Kay'La's help, I'm not sure what I would do. I never thought that as a new supervisor, I'd have to deal with so many complicated problems. I expected tricky customer service situations, but I guess I didn't really understand just how much time and effort I'd have to spend on the 'people' side of things".

As Kay'La's smiling face appeared on the screen, Kevin breathed a sigh of relief.

"I'm glad to see you", Kay'La said. "I know it's been quite a week". Although Kay'La normally checked in with Kevin once a week, on Friday, it was Thursday, and she'd already spoken to him every day. "Checking in with people more often when things are tough is the kindest thing to do", Kay'La thought to herself. Turning her full attention to Kevin, she said, "Update me on what's happened since we talked yesterday. I'm all ears". Kevin took a deep breath and said, "I think things are going a little better today than they were yesterday. Cindy is back at her desk today and everyone has been kind to her". "I'm glad to hear that", said Kay'La. "She's been through a lot too. It's easy to be blame people and be angry with them, but when people are acting out of fear, there's no telling what they will do. You did the right thing when you knocked on Cindy's car window and asked if she needed help".

Last week, as Kevin was heading home, he had passed Cindy's car in the parking lot and was surprised to see her sitting behind the wheel crying. He wasn't sure what to do, because Cindy had been in an even worse mood than usual for the past few weeks. But it seemed so out of character for her that he decided to knock on her window and see if she needed help. To his surprise, he found out that she was in tears because she was just found out she hadn't been promoted to Regional Manager. "I really needed this promotion, and I didn't get it because I wasn't ranked highly enough in the performance grids. I had the interview of my life, and the hiring manager even told me I interviewed the best, but the performance scores are the most important thing at this company, I guess", Cindy said. "My husband has been laid off for the past year and hasn't been able to find another job. My house is about to be foreclosed on, and I don't know how to tell my kids any of this. I don't have any other family here and it's just too much pressure. The stress of competing for this job is just killing me. I'm sure I shouldn't be telling you this, but I'm at the end of my rope".

After Cindy calmed down, Kevin headed to his car. "No wonder she always seems to be in a bad mood", he thought to himself. "That's a lot to bear". Before heading home, Kevin decided to call Kay'La on the phone. He wasn't sure what to do, but the one thing he was certain of was that he needed advice. After he told Kay'La everything that had happened, she said "Kevin, that was the right thing to do and very kind of you. And thank you for calling me. No one in this company should have to bear that kind of burden and live in fear. I didn't realize that Cindy and her family have been struggling with so much. Even though she didn't get the promotion, Cindy doesn't have to worry, here's what Codstom can do to help… ".

Now It's Your Turn to Reflect and Apply

Put on your Leader Hat and think about what you would do if you were in Kay'La's position. How could you help your organization reduce the fear that comes from competition? How could you encourage collaboration, cooperation and kindness instead? Write your ideas here:

Chapter 7 Kind-Points

- *The Kind Leadership Continuum.* Modeling and helping people learn kinder ways to *interact* is just as important for a Kind Leader as acting, reacting and leading by kind example. As leaders become kinder they are able to help people move from competition and fear on the far left-hand side of the Continuum to the increasing trust and unity that comes with collaboration, cooperation and finally full Kindness on the right hand side.
- *Competition.* Competition and competitive interactions are based on winning and losing. The possibility of losing causes a lot of fear. Because fear and trust don't go together, competition and competitive interactions aren't conducive to kindness. Practicing kind leadership helps leaders move people and organizations away from competitive interactions towards collaboration and cooperation.
- *Collaboration.* Collaboration is a kinder way of interacting than competition. In collaborative interactions, although people still work primarily separately, they are beginning to trust each other and work together. Bargaining behaviors and language such as 'buy-in' and 'compromise' are common, and people still put their own needs before those of others.
- *Cooperation.* Cooperative interactions are even kinder than collaborative ones, and are based on 'win–win' and mutual benefit. In cooperative interactions, people put others' needs first and come together to serve another. Although there are still two or more sides, there aren't losers, buy-in or compromises. Both collaborative interactions and cooperative ones are reasons to celebrate and 'recognize' people for their efforts to work together.
- *Beyond 'win–win': Kindness.* The last stage of The Kind Leader ship Continuum is aspirational: Kindness. It is the stage in which two sides no longer exist, and like a beautiful symphony, people come together in harmony. In Kindness, people aren't separate, but interconnected in 'oneness'. Like an orchestra's conductor, Kind Leaders can both imagine a world of kindness and help people come together beautifully to create it.

Notes

1 "Compete". *Merriam-Webster.com Dictionary*, www.merriam-webster.com/dictionary/compete. Accessed January 19, 2021.
2 If you are silently thinking to yourself that this is impossible because people won't do their best and put in the time and effort to do the work if they know they aren't be graded on results, please 'check your thinking' and reflect on why you believe that competition is the only way to motivate people.
3 "Collaborate". *Merriam-Webster.com Dictionary*, www.merriam-webster.com/dictionary/collaborate. Accessed January 19, 2021.
4 "Cooperate". *Merriam-Webster.com Dictionary*, www.merriam-webster.com/dictionary/cooperate. Accessed January 19, 2021.
5 Karyn Ross, Tough Times Require Lean – And a Little Creativity, *ISE Magazine*, July 2020, p. 33.
6 My father, Saul Ross, was a professor of physical education. He didn't focus on competition though, he focused on cooperation and play. To learn more about the benefits of cooperating instead of competing in play, please visit his colleague, Terry Orlick's Cooperative Games website: https://cooperativegames.com/tag/terry-orlick/
7 Andrea Medea, *Conflict Unraveled: Fixing Problems at Work and in Families*, PivotPoint Press, 2004, p. 182.
8 Excerpt from John Paul Lederach, *The Moral Imagination*,. Apple Books, 2005. https://books.apple.com/us/book/the-moral-imagination/id782981677
9 Karyn Ross, Beyond Win–Win Solutions, Class Paper for MLS 558, May 2008. A special thanks to Professor Laura Noah for inspiring me to continue working on creating what lies beyond 'win–win'.

Chapter 8

When Things Don't Go Kindly

As leaders we have the opportunity to lead by our actions. We also have the opportunity to call out others who aren't, to point out to people how their unkind behaviors affect others.

Leslie Henckler, Service sector leader

Discussion: Kind Leadership Is the Answer

As I'm sure you've seen and experienced while wearing both your Leader and Follower Hats, unkindness is going to happen. Whether you are at work, at home or in the community, competition and competitive interactions between individuals and groups cause people to act, react and interact unkindly, and produce more competition and more fear. It's a vicious circle, further exacerbated by outdated traditional models of leadership.

Unkindness is also going to happen because people are people. As human beings people are hardwired for negativity bias, to assume 'negative intent', so it's difficult not to get involved in unkind ways of acting, reacting and interacting with others. And if people are in situations where leaders don't model kind behavior, or model unkind behavior, they themselves will take their cues from those leaders and imitate those unkind behaviors as well.

Finally, unkindness is going to happen because, as people, no one is perfect. Despite their best intentions and efforts, difficult, stressful

DOI: 10.4324/9781003141433-8

circumstances, like those everyone has experienced during the COVID-19 pandemic, are simply going to overwhelm their current level of practice and ability to be kind. If there is one thing that I can guarantee, it is that the people you lead are, at some point, going to be unkind, and that you as a leader, are going to be unkind as well. (I am too.) Kindness, leading by kind example and interacting kindly is something that each of us is going to have to practice for our entire lifetime. As a Kind Leader, you are going to stumble, and that's okay. As long as you pick yourself up, brush yourself off, spend some time reflecting, and get back up and start practicing again.

As a Kind Leader, because the fact that you will be dealing with unkind situations is certain, this Discussion section is all about what to do when the inevitable unkindness happens. How to act and react to get your people back on track and interacting more kindly. And how to get yourself back on track as well. Just like every other part of kind leadership, as I'm sure you won't be surprised to hear, it will take practice. The good thing is, that practice will help you better your ability to lead with kindness and it will lead to more kindness in the world!

The Top Three Reasons Unkindness Happens

For Kind Leaders having a clear understanding of the top three reasons why unkindness happens is extremely important. It doesn't matter where or in what situation and circumstance you are wearing your Leader Hat, those reasons are the same. They go together, and you might find one, two or all three at play when people are acting, reacting and interacting unkindly.

The first reason is that the overall organizational system itself promotes competition and a culture of fear. As you saw in Chapter 7, ends-focused, 'results-oriented' systems can pit group against group and person against person in competitive efforts to 'win'. When people are afraid of losing, they may act in unkind ways to other individuals and groups in order to increase their chances of winning and the others' chances of losing. Unfortunately, unkindness doesn't stop when a person or group wins, because the winner, afraid of the possibility of 'losing' next time, may continue to act unkindly in order to hang on to, or increase, their power. In organizations, this can be seen when salespeople who are competing to 'make their numbers', shout at members of the operations' teams who point out errors in client setup or the difficulty in fulfilling promises made by sales to clients. Team members who refuse to help other team members because it might take them away from their work and hurt 'their numbers' is another example. In the wider community, candidates of different political parties say unkind things about each in political advertisements. Those words are echoed and amplified by supporters on social media, which leads to arguments and division among friends and family members with different political beliefs and alliances. Escalating competition and fear of losing can even lead to violence between different sides. All because of a competitive system that both creates and results in fear about what will happen to the other side when one side wins and is in power. More broadly, systemic racism, violence against minority groups, lack of sharing between those that 'have' and those that 'don't' are all examples of terrible unkind outcomes that are a result of systemic competition and a culture of fear.

The second reason is that most organizations don't have clear definitions and standards, set by leadership about what kind actions, reactions and interactions look like. To understand this, take a moment and put on your Follower Hat. Think about your organization's values. (If you aren't sure what they are, look them up on the intranet. The fact that you don't know them off by heart is the first sign that what those values 'look like' in action hasn't been made clear. If your organization doesn't have a list of values, go back to Chapter 2, page 21 and take a look at the list of the most commonly used words in values statements.) Now, choose one value and think about the actual behaviors that your leaders have specifically defined as ways that people need to act and react that 'show' this value. Next, search your intranet to find where those definitions and descriptions are housed. If you can't do it, I'm not surprised, because although most organizations have values' statements that use words such as integrity, honesty and respect, the specific *behaviors* of how people should act, react and interact to model those values are rarely defined. Now, if your company has a dress code, search your intranet and see what you find. Chances are there are both descriptions in words and pictures of what is acceptable and what isn't so that people can easily see if their wardrobe choice is within the standard. Because people come from different backgrounds and experiences they have different ideas of what 'acting with integrity' looks like. Just like a company dress code, organizations need to have kind ways of acting, reacting and interacting clearly defined, in words and pictures, for all to see and understand.[1]

The third reason is that the leader of the organization and system isn't modeling kind behavior themselves. As you've seen throughout this book, followers take their cues about how to act, react and interact from their leaders. If their leader doesn't model kind behavior, or actively models unkind behavior, then that is what followers will do as well. This last reason ties directly back to the first: Because leaders, as people, are parts of organizational systems that promote competition and cultures of fear, they themselves are just as likely to be caught up in those vicious cycles as anyone else. As you saw in Chapter 3, the child who is yelled at and treated unkindly because their parent's leader treats them unkindly, will grow up to lead in exactly the same way. Leaders are educated with traditional competitive models and mentored by leaders with those same experiences. That's why changing the overall leadership model and system to kind leadership is so important. Kind leadership is the answer to breaking the cycle of fear and creating new kind ways of acting, reacting and interacting that will spread kindness throughout the world.

KLC Stop & Think Point: How conscious are you of the effects of traditional leadership models and cycles of fear in your own leadership choices on a day-to-day basis? Put on your Leader Hat and reflect on how you can be more conscious of those effects so that you can actively work to break the cycle.

As a Kind Leader, recognizing when things are going unkindly, and then helping people change their actions, reactions and interactions from unkind to kind ones is the way you will actively break the cycle and create a kinder world. In the next section, you'll learn about the five steps to take when things don't go kindly.

The Five Steps Kind Leaders Take When Things Don't Go Kindly

When things don't go kindly, leaders have an opportunity to break the cycle of fear, help people learn how to act and react more kindly and move interactions to the right on The Kind Leadership Continuum. Using The Five Steps Kind Leaders Take When Things Don't Go Kindly will both help people learn to practice kindness and it will also help you, as a Kind Leader, deepen your practice. It's important that you don't shy away from situations where unkindness occurs, but use them instead as an opportunity to actively lead by kind example.

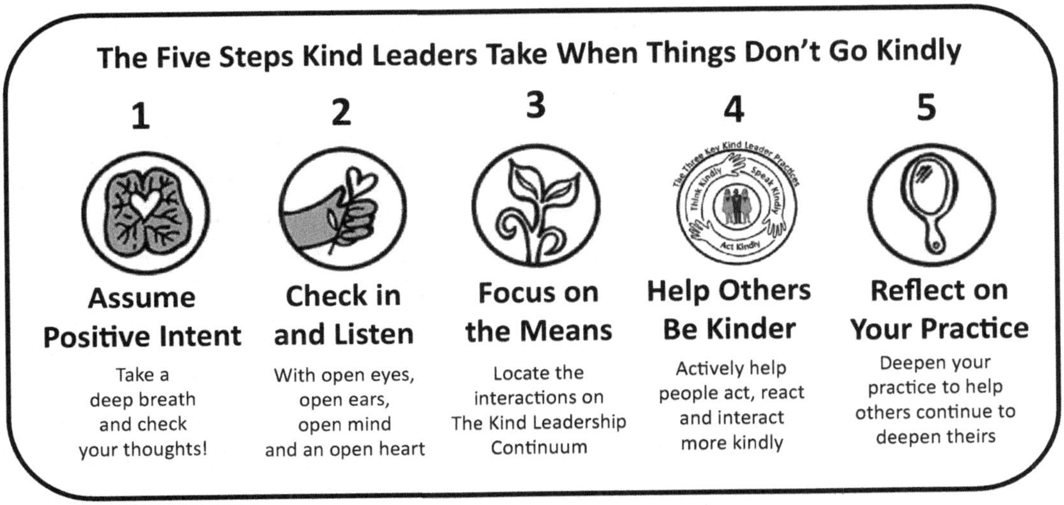

The Five Steps Kind Leaders Take When Things Don't Go Kindly

1	2	3	4	5
Assume Positive Intent	**Check in and Listen**	**Focus on the Means**	**Help Others Be Kinder**	**Reflect on Your Practice**
Take a deep breath and check your thoughts!	With open eyes, open ears, open mind and an open heart	Locate the interactions on The Kind Leadership Continuum	Actively help people act, react and interact more kindly	Deepen your practice to help others continue to deepen theirs

Figure 8.1 What Kind Leaders do when unkindness happens.

The Five Steps Kind Leaders Take When Things Don't Go Kindly are (1) Assume Positive Intent, (2) Check-in and Listen, (3) Focus on the Means, (4) Help Others Be Kinder and (5) Reflect on Your Own Practice. I'll give you a short description of each and then give you examples of how to use them in unkind situations.

1. *Assume Positive Intent*: The first step to take when things don't go kindly is to *assume positive intent*, the first Think Kindly behavior. Because of negativity bias, and the effects of competition and cycles of fear, when you see people acting, reacting and interacting unkindly, it's very easy to automatically assume the worst instead of the best. Think back to Michelle's story in Chapter 5 about team members saying unkind things about each other. When Michelle heard others speaking unkindly it was easy for her get pulled into negative assumptions. As a Kind Leader, when faced with unkind actions and interactions, understand that your first impression will likely be negative. Take a few minutes (and some deep breaths!) and deliberately and consciously work to assume positive intent. This will help you have an open mind and open heart when you go to check in to learn more about the situation.

2. *Check-in and Listen*: Step two is to go check in with people so that instead of assuming, you can actually see and hear what is going on. Go to where the unkindness is occurring and see for yourself. If a team member is being unkind to another, if you haven't already observed the unkindness, go to where the team members work and see for yourself. If two departments, like Sales and Service, are interacting unkindly, go to both areas, and check in with everyone involved. While you are checking in with people, watch their body language and listen to the words they are choosing (both denotative and connotative meanings) and to their tone of voice. Ask questions to gain a better understanding of how each person involved is feeling and doing. Open your mind and heart so that you can see and hear what people are afraid of and why. Then focus on the 'means', what is happening inside the organization and in people's lives that is resulting in their unkind actions, reactions and interactions.

3. *Focus on the Means*. Once you've checked in with people and listened to understand what they are afraid of and why, locate their interactions on The Kind Leadership Continuum. Are their unkind actions and reactions stemming from fear of not receiving a promotion? Are people 'throwing others under the bus', so that they are ranked higher than others on their performance review? When you see and hear this you can be pretty sure people are in the Competition part of The Kind Leadership Continuum. Are people 'strong-arming' others to coerce them into buying-in to a solution that they aren't comfortable with? Is it causing unkindness and disagreement between teams who are supposed to be working together? Then likely they are on the collaboration part of the Continuum. Once you're confident that you understand why people are afraid, and where they are on The Kind Leadership Continuum, the next step is to decide what to do and then do it!

4. *Help Others Be Kinder*. As you've learned throughout this book, kind leadership is about action. It's about modeling kind behavior and leading by kind example so that others can learn how to be kinder. Just thinking about how to help people act, react and interact more kindly isn't going to help *them* and it's not going to break the cycle of fear. Once you've decided why people are acting unkindly,

spend time helping them practice acting, reacting and interacting more kindly. If someone is speaking unkindly to another, using words and phrases that aren't acceptable, make sure the person knows words that are acceptable and then make sure the person uses those words instead. Spend time working with a team to help them learn how to consider others outside of themselves first, so that they move from collaborative to cooperative ways of working. From 'buy-in' to 'win–win'. Sometimes, you won't be sure what to do to help others act, react and interact more kindly. And that's okay. Because the solution to many manifestations of unkindness, especially those that are parts of long-standing, seemingly intractable cycles of fear, aren't easy. Working with others on figuring out kinder ways and trying them out will be the best way for all involved to learn. And please don't forget to recognize everyone's efforts to be kinder. Including your own. Which brings us to the last of the Five Steps.

5. *Reflect on Your Practice*: Followers take their cues about how to act, react and interact from their leaders, so it's important to recognize unkindness is a sign that you need to reflect on your own actions, reactions and interactions as a leader. What are you modeling for the people you are leading? Have you clearly defined what words and actions are acceptable and those that aren't? Can people easily find those definitions? In the past, when you've seen unkindness, have you just let it pass, or have you deliberately chosen to help people become kinder? If you chose to let it go in the past, what will you do differently now and in the future? Are you still being unconsciously influenced by traditional leadership models based on competition? In order to break the cycles of competitive interaction and fear, you are going to have to deepen your practice as a Kind Leader. Moving people along the Continuum toward trust and Kindness starts and ends, with you. The more you practice and lead by kind example, the more your followers will as well when they wear their Leader Hats.

KLC Stop & Think Point: Do you notice situations where your people are acting, reacting and interacting unkindly? Put on your Leader Hat and think about how you can be more deliberate in looking for unkindness at work, at home and in the wider community.

As a leader, if you think that helping people act, react and interact more kindly is going to be a lot of work and take up a lot of your time, you are right. Maybe you are thinking to yourself, "How will I get my own work done, and how will I make sure that all our organization's priorities are met if I spend my time helping people figure out how to be kinder?" If that's the case, it's okay. Remind yourself that one of the big differences between traditional leadership models and kind leadership is the focus on the means – *how we get there* – first, rather than on *where we are going*. As a leader, spending your time focusing on the means, on others, on helping your people learn to be kinder, as people, will ensure that the 'ends', a kinder world, where people trust and help each other, turns out right.

In the next section, you'll hear about how three different leaders practiced the Five Steps in three unkind situations. To better understand how you handle unkindness when you see it now, go to this chapter's Practice Section and complete the exercise (Figure 8.2) on page 180. (You can stop and do the exercise now or continue reading and do it at the end of this chapter.)

True Stories of Unkindness and What Kind Leaders Did about It

As I said at the beginning of this chapter, and as I know you've experienced, unkindness is going to happen. In organizations, at home, in communities and in the world. You don't have to look far to find examples. In this section you'll learn about three leaders who made the choice to lead by kind example and follow the Five Steps to create kinder outcomes, break the cycle of fear and move their people, and their organization, closer to true Kindness.

Story #1: Think Kindly

Matthew Grant is a communications leader. When he began a new position, one of the first things that he did was start regular check-ins to get to know his team. As he spent time with one of the managers, he noticed that they seemed to make a lot of negative assumptions about people and why work wasn't completed in a timely manner or to the standard the manager expected. Matthew also noticed that the manager often assumed 'negative intent' about what others were thinking, which affected how the manager acted and reacted to other team members, and how the whole team interacted together. During one conversation, the manager complained bitterly about one team member and the negative motives that they assumed the person had.

After taking a deep breath and checking his own thoughts, Matthew decided that he would *assume positive intent*. He hadn't been with the team very long and what he really needed to do was find out more. Matthew set up a special *check-in* with the manager to find out more about why they seemed so negative, and then he *listened*. And what he heard surprised him. He realized that the manager didn't seem to know how to ask questions very well. So instead of checking in and asking people how they were doing, they just *assumed*. Because Matthew knew that the former leader of the organization encouraged competition and competitive interactions, Matthew wasn't surprised that the manager had a tendency to assume negative intent. They were on the far left of The Kind Leadership Continuum, and caught up in a cycle of fear. So here's what Matthew decided to do. He helped the manager craft some open-ended questions that would help them learn more, instead of assuming, and he practiced the following phrase with the manager: "Wouldn't it be nice if we had the answers to these questions?" Then he helped the manager set up a schedule of check-ins where they could ask people the questions they had prepared instead of assuming. Matthew thanked the manager for their willingness to try new ways of acting and interacting and continued to schedule regular check-ins to help the manager make further progress.

On reflecting on his own practice, Matthew realized that it takes a lot of time and effort to learn, and that as a leader new to the organization, he was going to have to look and listen carefully, check-in and continue to recognize his people's efforts. Through constant practice, they would all make progress on being kinder, together.[2]

Story 2: Speak Kindly

Stéfany Oliver leads a team that improves processes in a government agency. One day she was copied on a group email string that included a person she didn't know personally and who was new to the agency. As Stéfany read the email, she noticed herself starting to get upset because some of the references the person was making to improvement tools and processes didn't align with her own views and felt unkind. At first, Stéfany thought about writing back to the person, but hesitated and *checked her thoughts* instead. As she reflected, Stéfany realized that she, herself, was assuming negative intent and that she needed to *consciously change her thoughts to kind ones* and *assume positive intent* before proceeding any further.

After spending some time thinking about what to do, Stéfany decided that instead of stating her concerns about the person's perspective on the group email, she would ask if they were open to connecting and talking by phone. Because of coronavirus, it wasn't possible to meet in person, and Stéfany knew that if they continued communicating by email, she wouldn't be able to hear the person's tone of voice and might interpret the words incorrectly. Stéfany was happy to find out that the person was willing to chat and they set up time to *check in*.

As Stéfany prepared for the conversation, she decided that instead of telling the person why she thought they were wrong, which could be confrontational and set up a competitive 'win–lose' situation, she would simply ask the person why they said what they did, and then *listen, with open eyes, open ears, open mind and an open heart*. Instead of focusing on the ends, and getting her point across, Stéfany decided to focus on the means so that she could get to know the person and understand where they were coming from.

After the conversation, Stéfany sent me an excited note! After an hour-long discussion, Stéfany found out that she and the person really had very similar views, not different ones. Because of assumptions both people were making, they had misinterpreted each other's views in the email string. By the end of the conversation, instead of interacting competitively, they decided to start a friendship and work together cooperatively to serve their organization.

Reflecting on her own practice, Stéfany realized that email wasn't a good way to communicate, especially if feelings and emotions were involved. In future, she decided to make sure to connect with people by phone and video chat (or in person) whenever she felt uncomfortable with anything she saw in email conversations.[3]

Story 3: Act Kindly

Ann Howell, who you've met in earlier chapters, is a leadership coach and consultant with years of experience. During her Kind Leader interview, she told me about an experience she had while she was a leader in a multinational organization. A person had been hired to be a peer of Ann's, but people on that person's team didn't seem to like her. The person's new teammates spoke unkindly to their new colleague and didn't try to work collaboratively and cooperatively with her. Ann was frustrated because the manager of that team didn't do anything to stop the unkind behavior or help the person who was being treated unkindly.

As Ann watched the situation unfold, she spent time looking and listening carefully to what was going on. She assumed positive intent, that her peer was doing the best that she could to fit in and that the competitive nature of the team she was on wasn't helping her to succeed. She could also see that her peer felt upset and depressed and blamed herself for the situation. As a Kind Leader, Ann knew she couldn't let the situation continue. So she decided to act, and convinced the person to leave the team she was on and come and work for Ann instead. Ann didn't stop there, though. She spent time regularly checking in with and coaching her new team member on communication style and skills. Some of the feedback that Ann gave her team member was tough, but given in a kind way focused on the means and considering her team member's feelings and needs first. Ann knew that it would take a lot of time, consistent effort and guided practice to help her team member make the progress she needed, and Ann made the commitment to make and take that time.

"Years later, we're still friends", Ann told me at the end of the interview. A wonderful, kind end to a story that could, in many instances, and many organizations, have had a very different ending. In an organization, where leaders didn't notice unkindness and focused only on the ends, it's possible the person would have been fired. Then the fear and unhappiness they felt from that experience would be transferred to other parts of their life in a negative cycle of fear. Ann's kindness and kind leadership broke that cycle, and led instead to friendship, trust and unity.[4]

There's No Such Thing as 'Cruel To Be Kind' … If It's Not Kind, Don't Do It

As you read in the three stories above, responding to unkindness requires making a deliberate and conscious decision to spend your time and effort modeling kind ways to act, react and interact. One of the questions I'm often asked is:

> What about people who really are out to sabotage organizations? Who really do have negative intentions? And what about those people who just aren't suited for the job they are doing and no matter what you do,

> they just don't get better and don't get the hint that they're not wanted? Aren't there times when, as a leader, you really just have to be 'cruel to be kind'?

I'd like you to think about those words, and from what you've learned about kind leadership, The Kind Leadership Continuum and The Five Steps Kind Leaders Take When Things Don't Go Kindly, and take a moment to reflect. As a leader, if you are really focused on the means, consider others first, and actively model kind behavior to lead by kind example, 'being cruel to be kind' isn't even a possibility because fear and kindness can't exist together. Giving feedback to someone in an unkind way using unkind words doesn't create more kindness in the world. Or more trust. It creates fear. Simply firing someone whose work isn't up to standard doesn't help break the vicious cycle of fear. It only adds to it as the person takes out their unhappiness on others in other areas of their life.

As a Kind Leader, what should you do in the event one of your people is really acting from a place of negative intent? Here are a couple of suggestions. If you have done your best to assume positive intent, checked in and listened, and come to the conclusion that others or the person themself is in danger, contact the proper authorities, whether it be law enforcement, mental health professionals or both. Keeping the person, and others in your organization safe is a kind thing to do. If someone on your team or in your organization's work (ends and results) aren't up to standard, spend extra time focused on the means and figuring out how you can help them. I once worked in an organization where a long-term employee kept avoiding taking a professional development course that had a test at the end. The person's leader was very upset because the department's 'statistics' didn't look good as it was a required course. When I checked in with the person and listened with open eyes, open ears, open mind and an open heart, the person opened up to me and told me that they didn't know how to read. They were embarrassed to admit it and had developed such good strategies and coping mechanisms that they had, so far, been able to progress in their career without anyone noticing. Once the employee told the leader what the real problem was, accommodations were made to have the course and test read to the employee so they could be in compliance with the departmental requirement. The organization also arranged for the employee to see a reading specialist. The reading specialist diagnosed the employee with dyslexia and helped them learn to read. Not only was the person better able to do their job, they also were able to function better in their life and get help for their child who happened to have exactly the same struggle.

As a leader, you will find that many instances of unkindness are complicated. You will also find that responding with unkindness and 'being cruel to be kind' may seem to be an easier path. But in the end it's not, because 'you reap what you sow' and 'sow what you reap', and unkindness, and the problems it causes, will continue, at work, at home and in the wider world. If you find yourself thinking, "This is a situation in which I need to be 'cruel to be kind'", please take some time to check your thoughts and reflect, and work on *assuming positive intent*, the first of The Five Steps Kind Leaders Take When Things Don't Go Kindly.

Failures of Leadership and Failures of Kindness Have Terrible Consequences for Us All

In a chapter in the *Handbook of Conflict Resolution: Theory and Practice* called "Intractable Conflict", Peter T. Coleman describes intractable conflicts as those "that persist because they appear impossible to resolve".[5] He goes on to say that intractable conflicts differ from others in that they appear to be more persistent, destructive and resistant to resolution, and that most "don't begin as such, but become so as escalation, hostile interactions, sentiment, and time change the quality of the conflict".[6] Coleman adds other common characteristics of intractable conflicts are that "they are typically associated with cycles of high and low intensity and destructiveness, are often costly in both social and economic terms, and can become pervasive, affecting even mundane aspects of disputants' lives".[7] Although you might think to yourself, "I'm not involved in intractable conflicts in my organization. Those are things like wars in different regions of the world, and feuds that go on between families for generations. I'm just dealing with people being unkind to each other at work", when you really think about it, because followers in one organization wear Leader Hats in other areas of their life, when leaders fail to address unkindness in one place, that unkindness and it's resulting cycle of fear creates intractable conflicts that affect us all in many areas of life. Neighbors who have different political views who were once friends now look at each other with suspicion or are outright unkind to each other. People who spend their day in unkind work environments take out their feelings of frustration and fear on others in road-rage incidents on their commute home. People self-medicate their anxiety and depression from the fear that being in constant competition with others to have 'more' and 'be more' brings and then model those behaviors to their children. Although you might not have looked at it this way before, in effect all of us are living in situations involving intractable conflicts that seem impossible to solve; all because of failures of leadership and failures of kindness. When leaders don't actively look for and fail to respond to unkindness, the conditions for intractable conflict are created. The answer to this problem? Kind leadership. And Kind Leaders who recognize and realize that their role is not to shy away from dealing with unkindness as it occurs, but to use the Five Steps to solve the underlying problems and break the cycle of fear that leads to intractable conflict.

Before ending this Discussion section and starting the Practice one, a quick reminder that often, large, seemingly intractable problems are made up of a lot of small ones. As a Kind Leader, every unkindness, no matter how small, that you help resolve, goes a long way to both moving people from the left-hand side of The Kind Leadership Continuum, and also to helping people learn how they can use the Five Steps when things don't go kindly when they wear their Leader Hat. Your efforts to use the Five Steps are leading to a kinder world for all.

Practice: Practical Exercises to Use to Turn Your Thoughts into Action

It's easy to get caught up in unkindness at work, at home and in your community. The best antidote? Practicing The Five Steps Kind Leaders Take When Things Don't Go Kindly. The more you practice, the more habitual the Five Steps will become. Because it's so important to practice, I suggest copying the third exercise into a notebook and recording your practice for as long as it takes to become comfortable with it. And if you find yourself slipping back at any time, start recording again!

Exercise 1: How Do You Respond To Unkindness Currently?

As a leader, unkindness is going to happen because your people are people and respond to competition and cycles of fear with unkindness. How you respond to that unkindness will help people learn to be kinder, and break those cycles of fear. What do you do as a leader now when you see unkindness? How do you respond currently? You'll use the situations you write about here in the next exercise as well.

How do you respond to unkindness now? With you Leader Hat on, think about three different recent situations in which you noticed unkindness. Record what you saw in the situation and what you did, even if you did nothing. In the next exercise you'll apply the five steps to these situations.	
Describe the unkindness	**What I did**
Situation 1:	
Situation 2:	
Situation 3:	

Figure 8.2 What do I do now when I see unkindness?

Exercise 2: How Could You Have Used the Five Steps to Respond Differently?

Now that you're familiar with the Five Steps, reflect on the situations you described above. What could you have done differently? How could that have helped your people learn how to act, react and interact more kindly?

How could I have used The Five Steps to respond instead? With you Leader Hat on think about how you could apply The Five Steps to the situations that you wrote about in Exercise 8.1. Can you go back to the people in those situations and help them now?	
Describe the unkindness	**How I could have used the five steps**
Situation 1:	
Situation 2:	
Situation 3:	

Figure 8.3 How could I have used the five steps instead?

Exercise 3: Deliberately Practicing the Five Steps

Actively look for unkindness in your organization, at home and in your community. Use the Five Steps to take action! Write about what happens during each step here:

1. Assume Positive Intent (Take a deep breath and check your thoughts)

2. Check-in and Listen (With open eyes, open ears, open mind and an open heart)

3. Focus on the Means (Locate the interactions on The Kind Leadership Continuum)

4. Help Others Be Kinder (Actively help people act, react and interact more kindly)

5. Reflect on Your Practice (Deepen your practice to help others deepen theirs)

Reflection: What Would You Do? Kind Leader Practice Scenarios

Now that you've had the opportunity to read the ideas and theory presented in the Discussion section and do the Practice exercises, it's time to reflect on what you've learned and proactively plan how to apply those learnings.

This book is almost finished, and so is Kay'La Janson's and Kevin Landrell's story. Let's check in with each of them and see what they've learned …

Kind Leadership Is the Answer to Creating a Culture of Trust

Scenario 1 – Kay'La's Story: It's Not the End, It's Just the Beginning!

Kay'La Janson closed her laptop and checked her watch. It was five-thirty and time to head home for the day. As she put her laptop into her bag, Kay'La thought to herself, "I can't believe a year has passed! It seems like I just got to Codstom. But the calendar doesn't lie! It's a year to the day!" As Kay'La walked out of her office, she smiled at the vases of flowers lined up on Anderson's desk. "Don't worry, don't worry, I know it's time to go home. I'm just packing up", Anderson said. "I could hardly see you through the flowers", said Kay'La. "Isn't it amazing", said Anderson. "Flowers, cards, handwritten notes, and that wonderful video message the Executives put together! They were so funny! In all the years I've been here before you were CEO Kay'La, nothing like this ever happened. People are so much happier now! It's amazing what a little kindness can do!" "It's what I took this job for, Anderson", Kay'La replied. "No one should have to work in fear. And what people learn at work, they bring home, and then they live in fear there as well. Taking this job was the best decision I ever made, and I couldn't have done it without you, Anderson. We're a great team and I appreciate you more than words can say!"

Kay'La took the elevator down to the first floor, and as she headed to the door, everyone she passed smiled and said, "Hey Kay'La! Have a great evening. See you tomorrow!" Kay'La knew everyone by name and took the opportunity to ask each person how they were doing and how their day had been. Sitting in her car, as she put on her seatbelt, Kay'La had a flashback to the first morning she'd arrived at Codstom. "All those angry faces", she thought to herself. "No one recognized them as people; no wonder they never looked up from the ground. Anderson was right. It's amazing what a little kindness can do. What a great first year, and the best thing about it is it's not the end, it's only the beginning!"

Scenario 2 – Kevin's Story: Everything Is Kind in the End. If It Isn't Kind, It's Not the End!

Kevin leaned back in his chair. Looking around at his team, he heard the pleasant tones that people were talking to clients with and he saw the smiles on people's faces. The best thing was that customer complaints had dropped dramatically and the fewer complaints customers made, the happier his team had become. And he was so proud of Molly and Jaden. They'd worked together and turned what they'd learned about making customers happy into a Positivity Program that was being used by customer service representatives throughout the whole company. It was hard to believe that two people who hadn't been able to get along for more than five minutes a year ago, could become such good friends. "It's really unbelievable", Kevin thought to himself. But he knew it was true. And that he couldn't have done it without Kay'La's help. "Having someone to show me how to be a better, kinder leader really made a huge difference. And Kay'La's kind leadership didn't just help me be a better leader, it's helped everyone on my team, and my customers too, because when I help others, they're kinder to other people too. The kinder my team is, the happier customers are and the whole effect spreads".

Just as Kevin was about to turn back to his computer to log into his weekly check-in with Kay'La (he was excited to wish her happy one year anniversary today), Cindy Yang passed by on her way back to her office from the staff lounge. "Hi Kevin", she called cheerfully, "Have you talked with Kay'La yet today? Don't forget that it's her Codstom anniversary! The branch sent her flowers and she sent a picture of her holding them!" "I'm just about to call her", Kevin answered. "Even Cindy is happy now", Kevin thought to himself. The Leadership Development Mentoring program Kay'La had created was really working. Cindy treated people like people now, and she knew that at the end of the program, she'd be ready to be a Regional Manager. "It's been a great first year being a supervisor", Kevin thought to himself. "And best thing is, it's not the end, it's only the beginning. With Kay'La and Cindy's help, things can only get better. It's amazing what a huge difference a little bit of kindness makes".

Now It's Your Turn to Reflect and Apply

Looking backward: This is the last chapter in Kay'La and Kevin's fictional story (for now anyways!). And this is the last chapter in The Kind Leader book. Take some time to reflect on what you've learned about yourself, kindness and leadership, while reading. What steps have you already taken to turn what you've read into action? What happened? Write your reflections here:

Looking forward: Now, it's time to look (and move) forwards. Remember, Kind Leadership is about action. How are you going to begin your practice and lead with kindness? If you have already started practicing, what are your next steps? How will you deepen your practice? Write about your next steps and longer term plans here:

Chapter 8 Kind-Points

- *The top three reasons unkindness happens.* Unkindness is inevitable for three reasons. The first is that overall organizational systems promote competition and a culture of fear. The second is that the leaders of most organization don't set clear definitions and standards about what kind actions, reactions and interactions look like. The third reason is that the organization's leader isn't modeling kind behavior themselves, which ties back to the first reason.
- *Kind Leaders actively look for unkindness.* In traditional leadership models, leaders are responsible for 'ends' and 'results'. Traditional leaders may shy away from looking for unkindness because only the ends are important, not how they are achieved. Kind Leaders need to spend time looking for unkindness and then helping people learn to act, react and interact more kindly even though it takes a lot of time and effort.
- *Kind Leaders use the Five Steps to help people act, react and interact more kindly.* The Five Steps Kind Leaders Take When Things Don't Go Kindly are: (1) Assume Positive Intent: Take a deep breath and check your thoughts; (2) Check-in and Listen: With open eyes, open ears, open mind and an open heart; (3) Focus on the Means: Locate the interactions on The Kind Leadership Continuum; (4) Help Others Be Kinder: Actively help people act, react and interact more kindly; and (5) Reflect on Your Practice: Deepen your practice to help others continue to deepen theirs.
- *There's no such thing as 'cruel to be kind'.* Fear and kindness don't go together. As a leader, although it may seem easier to give feedback unkindly or to shy away from dealing with incidents of unkindness, if you find yourself thinking to yourself "I need to be cruel to be kind", then you need to rethink how you are dealing with the unkindness. Follow the Five Steps instead.
- *Kind leadership is the answer to solving seemingly intractable problems.* Because followers in one organization wear Leader Hats in other areas of their life, when leaders fail to address unkindness in one place, that unkindness and it's resulting cycle of fear creates intractable conflicts that affect us all in many areas of life. The answer is Kind Leaders who use the five steps to solve the underlying problems and break the cycles of fear that lead to intractable conflict.

Notes

1 This is a great activity to do at home as well. Family members may think they are acting, reacting and interacting kindly, but if there are no standards for what those actions 'look' like, they may think the behaviors they are exhibiting are kind, but they may not be.
2 Personal Interview with Matthew Grant on October 27, 2020.
3 Personal conversation with Stéfany Oliver on October 26, 2020.
4 Personal interview with Ann Howell on October 17, 2020. Please see the Resource Section at the back of this book for a link to Ann's Kindness Experiment blog series.
5 Peter T. Coleman, "Intractable Conflict" in Morton Deutsch et al., eds., *The Handbook of Conflict Resolution: Theory and Practice*, 2nd edition, Jossey-Bass, San Francisco, CA, 2006, p. 534.
6 Ibid., p. 534.
7 Ibid., p. 534.

Conclusion

If only we are brave enough to see it. If only we are brave enough to be it.
Amanda Gorman, Youth Poet Laureate

The Time for Kind Leadership Is Now

It's February 1, 2021, and as I sit down to write today, here's what I am thinking about:

- Almost seven hundred million people (about 9 percent of the world's population) go hungry each day. That number grows every year, and at the current rate, by 2030, there are likely to be more than 840 million people starving.[1]
- In 2020, in the US alone, more than 19,000 people died from gun violence, an almost 25 percent increase over 2019.[2]
- Around the world, 780 million people don't have access to clean water, and about 2.5 billion people (about 35 percent of the world's population) don't have access to proper sanitation.[3]
- More than 800,000 children, mostly from developing countries, aged five years and younger die from diarrhea each year because of unsafe drinking water.[4]
- Almost 44 percent of the world lives in poverty, on less than $5.50 per day.[5]
- Half of the poor are children. Women represent a majority of the poor in most regions. About 70 percent of poor people around the world aged fifteen and over have no schooling or only some basic education.[6]

DOI: 10.4324/9781003141433-9

- More than 40 percent of those living in poverty live in places negatively affected by conflict and violence.[7]

I could go on. Climate change. Systemic racism. Discrimination. Bullying. And what do all these seemingly intractable problems have in common? At their most basic, they are the result of failures of leadership and failures of kindness.

Failures of leadership because traditional models focused on competition and end-results perpetuate competitive interactions in which 'winners' hold all the power and resources, and the losers live in fear. Failures of leadership that create vicious cycles of fear and seemingly intractable conflicts.

Failures of kindness because leaders think first of themselves, instead of others, condone and promote unkind behaviors and don't model ways to think, speak and act kindly so that those who follow them can themselves learn to think, speak and act kindly as well.

Looking at the list, maybe you feel discouraged and hopeless. I don't. I feel encouraged.

Why? Because of *you*. You've finished reading this book and now you know how to use The Three Key Kind Leader Practices and their Key Behaviors to help your people learn to act and react more kindly. Because of what *you* practice and model, when your people wear their Leader Hats, they'll imitate the way that you lead by kind example. I'm encouraged because as you practice kind leadership, you'll help move your people along The Kind Leadership Continuum away from competitive interactions and fear toward collaborative, cooperative and kind ones. Then they'll spread those ways of interacting at home and in the community as well. I'm encouraged because every time you use The Five Steps Kind Leaders Take When Things Don't Go Kindly, you'll show people that seemingly intractable problems aren't. That by working together kindly, every single one of them can be solved.

I'm encouraged because now you have a different leadership model to use. A different model that focuses on the means, and on creating cultures of trust. A model in which kindness is synonymous with leadership.

Please start using it now. There's no need to wait to start leading by kind example. You don't have to be perfect. You just have to practice: every kind thought, word, act, every bit of leading with kindness will change the world for your followers and break the vicious unkind cycles of fear that people live and work in. Those cycles don't have to continue. You have a choice.

You can break the cycle. You can be the change. All you need to do is start. All it takes is your leadership and a little bit of kindness. Because even a little bit of kind leadership goes a long way.

It may be the end of the book, but it's just the beginning of a kinder world.

Thank you for your courage, commitment and kind leadership.

Let's get started!

Notes

1 www.worldvision.org/hunger-news-stories/world-hunger-facts Downloaded on 2/1/2021
2 www.npr.org/2021/01/03/952969760/2020-was-a-record-breaking-year-for-gun-related-deaths-in-the-u-s Downloaded February 1, 2021.
3 www.cdc.gov/healthywater/global/wash_statistics.html Downloaded on February 1, 2021.
4 Ibid.
5 www.worldbank.org/en/topic/poverty/overview Downloaded on February 1, 2021.
6 Ibid.
7 Ibid.

Glossary

Leader: A person who has at least one person following them.

Follower: A person who has decided to pay attention to, take their cues about how to act and react from, and have their thoughts, words and actions influenced by, a person they deem as 'leader'.

Empathy: The ability to sense other people's emotions, coupled with the ability to imagine what someone else might be thinking or feeling.[1]

Compassion: A sense of concern that arises when we are confronted with another's suffering and feel motivated to see that suffering relieved.[2]

Kindness: An action (or set of actions), connecting a person's internal feelings of empathy and compassion to others that is undertaken with the purpose of generating a positive effect and outcome for another.

Leading by kind example: Purposefully acting and reacting with kindness to generate positive effects and outcomes for others.

Culture: The way things are expected and allowed to be done around here, including actions, reactions and non-actions.

Trust: Trust means that followers believe that leaders have their best interests at heart at all times.

Negativity Bias: The tendency not only to register negative stimuli more readily but also to dwell on these events.[3]

Unconscious (Implicit) Bias: Attitudes and beliefs that occur outside of our conscious awareness and control.[4]

Confirmation Bias: The tendency for people to give more weight to information or evidence that confirms their already existing beliefs. Its effect is amplified for issues that have a strongly charged emotional component.[5]

Selective Attention: The tendency for people only to pay attention to information that confirms what they already believe.[6]

Neuroplasticity: The ability of our brain to develop new neural pathways throughout our life.

Denotative: The denotative meaning of a word is the one found in the dictionary.

Connotative: The connotative meaning is the associations, emotions and feelings people perceive a word to have. Connotations can be negative, neutral or positive.

Competition: To strive consciously or unconsciously for an objective (such as position, profit, or a prize); be in a state of rivalry.[7]

Collaboration: Work jointly with others or together.[8] Collaborative interactions are defined by 'buy-in' and compromise.

Cooperation: To act or work with another or others; to associate with another or others for *mutual benefit*.[9] 'Win-win' is a common waying of describing cooperative interactions.

The Five Key Characteristics of a Kind Leader

1. *Actively* models kind behavior: The actions kind leaders choose (and those they don't) are based on thoughts and feelings of empathy and compassion.
2. *Deliberately* thinks, speaks and acts kindly: The deliberate choices kind leaders make have the underlying purpose of creating positive outcomes for others.
3. *Considers* others first: Kind leaders understand that each follower is a valuable human beings who will learn, grow and contribute their best when treated kindly in a culture of trust.
4. *Reflects* deeply about their actions: No one is perfect, so kind leaders reflect deeply to see where their actions may have focused solely on the ends and created fear in their followers.
5. *Focuses* on the means: Kind leaders focus their time and energy on creating conditions – the means – that help their followers do their best and be their best so that the end results can be achieved kindly.

The Three Key Kind Leadership Practices and Their Behaviors

1. Think Kindly
   1. *Always assume positive intent*
      - The first thoughts that come to a leader's mind in response to situations that occur are positive.
   2. *Check your thoughts frequently*
      - To see whether you are assuming positive intent or not, and the effects that your thoughts are having on you and on others.
   3. *Consciously change unkind thoughts to kind one*
      - Once you become aware of your unkind thoughts, you can make a conscious choice to change them to kind ones.

2. Speak Kindly
   1. *Choose your words kindly*
      - Kind words are: Human, Living, Organic, Trusting, Focused on the Means
   2. *Use a kind tone of voice*
      - Tone of voice includes your pitch, volume, speed and breath and influences how people perceive and interpret your words
   3. *If it's not kind, don't say it*
      - Unkind words and phrases hurt people. If your words will hurt someone, don't say them.

3. Act Kindly
   1. *Check in with people, not on them*
      - Get to know and care about your people as whole people, and spend time with them to see how they are feeling, how they are doing, and what help they need.
   2. *Listen: With open eyes, open ears, open mind and an open heart*
      - To see and hear what your people are telling you and to what your mind and heart are saying to do to help them.
   3. *Recognize others*
      - Thank people for their *efforts* on a daily basis (the means) and celebrate them for who they are as whole people.

The Kind Leadership Continuum

The continuum of how people's *interactions* become kinder as leaders practice the Three Key Kind Leadership practices and their behaviors. The four stages on The Kind Leadership Continuum are *Competition* (Two-sides – Division – Divisiveness – Fear – Distrust), *Collaboration* (Buy-in – Opt-Out – Two Sides – Compromise – Separate), *Cooperation* (Win-Win – Two sides – Commonality – Together but separate) and *Kindness* (Harmony – Connection – Unity – Together – As One).

The Five Key Steps Kind Leaders Take When Things Don't Go Kindly

1. *Assume positive intent:* Take a deep breath and check your thoughts!
2. *Check in and listen:* With open eyes, open ears, open mind and an open heart.
3. *Focus on the means:* Locate the interactions on The Kind Leadership Continuum.
4. *Help others be kinder:* Actively help people act, react and interact more kindly.
5. *Reflect on your practice:* Deepen your practice to help others continue to deepen theirs.

Notes

1 What Is Empathy? https://greatergood.berkeley.edu/topic/empathy/definition. Downloaded on November 27, 2020.
2 Thupten Jinpa, *A Fearless Heart: How the Courage to Be Compassionate Can Transform Our Lives*, as quoted from *The Book of Joy: Lasting Happiness in a Changing World*, Penguin, 2016, New York, p. 252.
3 www.verywellmind.com/negative-bias-4589618 Downloaded on October 16, 2020.
4 Ruhl, C. (2020, July 1). Implicit or Unconscious Bias. *Simply Psychology*. www.simplypsychology.org/implicit-bias.html Downloaded on December 21, 2020.
5 Iqra Noor, Confirmation Bias, www.simplypsychology.org/confirmation-bias.html Downloaded January 11, 2021.
6 We Only Hear What We Want to Hear, https://exploringyourmind.com/only-hear-want-hear/ Downloaded January 11, 2021.
7 "Compete." *Merriam-Webster.com Dictionary*, www.merriam-webster.com/dictionary/compete. Accessed January 19, 2021.
8 "Collaborate." *Merriam-Webster.com Dictionary*, www.merriam-webster.com/dictionary/collaborate. Accessed January 19, 2021.
9 "Cooperate." *Merriam-Webster.com Dictionary*, www.merriam-webster.com/dictionary/cooperate. Accessed 19 Jan. 2021.

Some Additional Resources to Help Deepen Your Practice

Online

- The Love and Kindness Project Foundation is my registered public charity that fosters projects creating love and kindness in the world. We are a grass-roots 'kindness raising' organization dedicated to spreading kindness person-to-person around the world! Please visit our website at www.loveandkindnessproject.org for free Kindness Mini-Poster downloads and information about how you can get involved. Follow us on LinkedIn and join our Facebook Group @TheKindlies to get a daily kindness prompt to use and share!
- Visit Ann Howell's website for a six-week long Kindness Experiment: www.scienceofworking.com/your-kindness-experiment-week-6-curb-judgmental-thinking/

Books

- Karyn Ross, *Think Kindly – Speak Kindly – Act Kindly: 366 Easy and Free Ideas You Can Use to Create a Kinder World … Starting Today!* The Love and Kindness Project Publishing, 2020, ISBN 9798605840046
- Karyn Ross, *Big Karma and Little Kosmo Help Each Other*, The Love and Kindness Project Publishing, 2019, ISBN 9781097959488
- His Holiness the Dalai Lama, Archbishop Desmond Tutu with Douglas Abrams, *The Book of Joy: Lasting Happiness in a Changing World*, Avery, 2016 ISBN 9780399185045

- Ajahn Brahm, *Kindfulness: Don't Just Be Mindful, Be Kindful*, Wisdom Publications, 2016, ISBN 9781614292166
- John Paul Lederach, *The Moral Imagination: The Art and Soul of Building Peace,* Oxford, 2005, ISBN 0195174542
- Andra Medea, *Conflict Unraveled: Fixing Problems at Work and in Families*, PivotPoint Press, 2004, ISBN 9780974580807
- Morton Deutsch et al. (eds.), *The Handbook of Conflict Resolution: Theory and Practice*, Jossey-Bass, 2006, ISBN 9780787980580

Index

Note: Page numbers in *italics* indicate figures.

Printed in the United States
by Baker & Taylor Publisher Services